1726

Angmering Park Field

East Preston 1759

Common
Eight acres
Eight Acres

Little hook
Three Acres
Four Acres
Field

Hentys acre
Great Lashmore
North Hurst
New Field
North 4 acre
Wigmore

rglaves croft
two acres
Kerns croft
Great hook
Little Lashmore
Middle
South Hurst
two acre
Four Acres
Middle 4 acre
Wigmore

Church Field
Pococks Field
Four acres
inner town field
Bayliss
Two acres
Town field
Hill croft
Five Acres
South
Mead Pots

Ingrams croft
hog croft
house croft

Barn Field
spring
acre croft
North Croft
West Norris Field
East Norris Field
Four Acres
Seventeen Acres

House Field
Three Acres
Bakers
Crocked croft
acre
Smith Shop croft
acre
North Eight Acres

Twenty Acres
House croft
Barn Field
Frise
Five Acres
Middle Eight Acres
Three acres
Nine Acres

Acres
Eight Acres
2 acres
2 acre croft
hogg brook

2 acres
Five Acres
West Eight Acres
South Eight Acres
Four Acres

Four Acres
Three Acres
Three Acres

Fourteen Acres
Three acres and half
4 acres Steet furlong
Five Acres
Twenty Acres

elve cres
Four Acres
Four Acres
Three acres
1 1/2 acre
Two acre croft
Pococks acre
Six Acre Piece

vets ld
Four Acres
Six Acres
Farm Field
Eight Acres
Nine Acres

Three Acres
Seven Acres

Eight
Four Acres
Four acres and half
Watch house croft

Sea Piece
Sea Piece
South Common

Fd

EAST PRESTON & KINGSTON

An Illustrated History

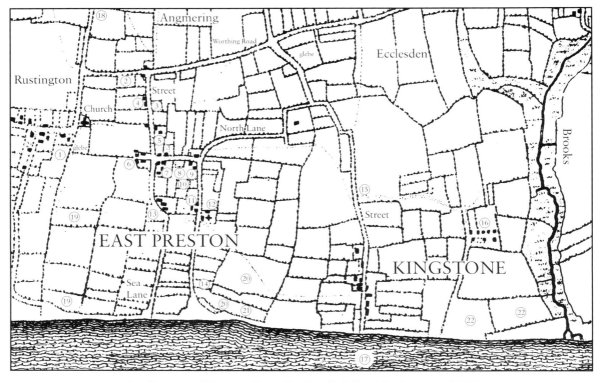

East Preston and Kingston villages. Based on Yeakell and Gardner map of 1778

1 West Preston Manor	8 Workhouse	15 West Kingston or new	19 Willowhayne Estate
2 Corner House or	9 Winters	Kingston Manor	1930
Preston Place	10 Baytree Cottage	16 Kingston Manor or	20 Angmering on Sea 1913
3 Forge Cottage	11 Beehives	East Kingston	21 Club House
4 Wisteria	12 Homestead	17 Chapel Site	22 Kingston Gorse Estate
5 Baytrees	13 House on Bend	18 London Brighton and	
6 Manor House	14 Coastguard Cottage	South Coast Railway	
7 Old Yews	1822	Station 1846	

EAST PRESTON & KINGSTON
An Illustrated History

Richard W. Standing

Phillimore

2006

Published by
PHILLIMORE & CO. LTD
Shopwyke Manor Barn, Chichester, West Sussex, England
www.phillimore.co.uk

ISBN 1-86077-384-2
ISBN 13 978-1-86077-384-6

Printed and bound in Great Britain by
CAMBRIDGE PRINTING

Contents

List of Illustrations

Frontispiece: East Preston and Kingston Village map

ACKNOWLEDGEMENTS

The author is grateful to many people, past and present, for information and use of photographs and illustrations. Ivo Candy and Chris Walters for invaluable information and photographs of East Kingston and the Candy family, Nos 12, 101, 102, 103, 126, 141, D.J. Standing, for pen drawings of several houses, and architectural drawings, Nos 11, 44, 45, 46, 50, 53, 73, 85, 94, Martin Hayes and West Sussex County Library Service, www.westsussexpast.org.uk/pictures, for the 1840 church drawing by W.E. Partridge, dust cover and No 24. By permission of the British Library, Add 5677 f74, Add 5678 f9, the two 1791 drawings of the church, Nos 22, 23. Richard Childs and W.S.R.O. for assistance in research, and permission to include the petition No 7 Ep/I/49/34, 1851 Borrer church drawing, No 25 and 1856 workhouse drawing, No 60, and frontispiece map Yeakell and Gardner 1778. *Littlehampton Gazette* for No 159. The Church, Parish Council, Preservation Society, and numerous people and institutions in East Preston and Kingston providing information over the past thirty years. The photographers and artists are known in some other instances. H.W. Freeland of Angmering, No 26. P. Seifert of Germany, Nos 37, 132. R. Standing Nos 1, 2, 6, 15, 19, 28, 35, 36, 40, 41, 43, 52, 54, 55, 56, 57, 59, 72, 82, 90, 91, 98, 104, 105, 107, 118, 122, 123, 124, 125, 129, 130, 144, 146, 154, 156, 160, 162, 166. J. White of Littlehampton Nos 8, 9, 18, 29, 47, 49, 61, 63, 65, 68, 71, 79, 80, 87, 92, 95, 97. Gratitude also for the checking of copy by Margaret Gilbert and to Phillimore & Co for their expertise.

PREFACE

The central thread for the history of the two villages of East Preston and Kingston may be outlined very briefly. It begins with the foundation of Saxon England and Sussex fifteen hundred years ago, when Saxon mercenaries made the country their own. It is thought that many of the native British remained in Sussex, as a subjugated class, eventually to be absorbed into the English race.

The villages that evolved and populated the country were dependent on the lands they owned, providing a farming base that supported them for well over a thousand years. East Preston was extensive enough to sustain twenty to thirty families, but no more without inviting disaster. It is only in the last two centuries that new technology has ruptured this relationship. In the 21st century the balance of man and nature requires purposeful intent and a perspective beyond the next harvest year and far into the future.

Christianity returned to the land that was now England, and thereafter cultural life revolved about the Church. But, in this third millennium, these roots are withering, and English culture is being lost in the global village.

Parish Boundaries

East Preston and Kingston stand together, west and east against the sea, halfway between Worthing and Littlehampton. Amongst the smallest parishes in Sussex, they barely amount to 900 acres between them. Ferring Rife marks the eastern boundary, with Angmering to the north and Rustington west. The soil is predominantly brickearth, apart from the flood plain of the rife, and is good for farming and horticulture. Being on the coastal plain all parts are low-lying, and East Preston church is probably at the highest elevation at under 28ft, on the extreme western boundary. Ferring Rife was subject to flooding, and in 1988 large catchment ponds were dug on the west side.

It is impossible to walk the boundaries of the parishes in the old customary way, but a 1671 description of the manorial boundaries, which were the same as the parish, can be brought up to date, ignoring the small addition to East Preston made in 1985 when its northern boundary was advanced to the railway line.[1]

1 *Worthing Road east of Roundstone, c.1965, before housing development, when it was the ancient elm-bordered lane.*

The bounds of the parish: To the south the sea. Then its western boundary with Rustington is on the west side of Angmering Lane and along the churchyard wall and east side of Station Road. It then extends along the north side of Worthing Road, and encompasses the built area at Somerset Road in the east, and runs south along the west side of gardens in Golden Avenue to the sea at the east end of South Strand.

Kingston adjoins East Preston on the east, and its northern boundary is at a stream next to land once called the 'Lakes Of Ecclesden', along part of which runs Parsons Way footpath between East Preston and Ferring churches. The eastern boundary is Ferring Rife – although its course was modified early in the 20th century.[2] To the south is the sea.

Boundaries relate to parish responsibilities and rights, so that streams were shared, whereas roads were in the parish that had responsibility for their repair.

The original parishes were not quite so compact before the Divided Parishes Act of 1876.[3] In the woods, less than a mile north of the *Woodman's Arms* at Hammerpot, is Park Field, the former outlier of East Preston manor and parish. Many coastal villages had these outliers, often in the Weald, deriving from Saxon grazing rights. Angmering was peculiarly affected, with several detached portions of Rustington and Poling in its midst.

2 *Church and Parsons Way, 1964.*
A view from The Street of the meadows before development of Vicarage Lane. The church spire was removed in 1951.

LOCAL HISTORY SOURCES AND NOTES

Even villages such as East Preston and Kingston have considerable histories, but they can only be known from surviving and accessible sources. Uncatalogued documents in a private archive are as good as dead, which was the situation in the 1960s, whereas today the West Sussex Record Office has a hoard of catalogued material, some now transcribed from difficult old writing into legible type.

The first history of the village was written in 1947 for the Women's Institute, by Mrs Paget, wife of a churchwarden, and apart from its contemporary anecdotes it must now be considered unreliable.[1] A decade later, in 1956, the Women's Institute compiled another village record, covering 100 years, which has good material.[2] Then in 1960 East Preston Cricket Club published an excellent centenary history, albeit only of the previous 70 years. Since 1980 R.W. Standing has written several typescript books on aspects of village history, while D.P. Lee has recently given us *East Preston in old picture postcards*. But, as yet, there is no Victoria County History volume covering this area, apart from drafts.

It is in the last thirty years that most of what survives of the bedrock material has become available and transcribed. The history of East Preston and Kingston therefore derives from this small miscellany, but is far from complete. The more important records are mentioned here, being used extensively in the text.

Chief of these are the Tithe Maps and Apportionments made after 1836, at WSRO. These provide the pattern of land ownership and tenancy in the 19th century, giving us a key to earlier records.[3]

Probably the most important early document is the 1759 (c.1724 tenants) James Colebrooke estate map, covering both villages and manors. This was found in a drawer of a local house and now there are good photographic copies for study. It illustrates a pattern of farms deriving from a medieval community of common field and manor courts, when everyone owed service to the lord of the manor.[4] Later survey notes based on the map are also available.

Another step back in time takes us to 1671, and a similar survey of the manors, but in written form as a 'terrier'. This ponderous description of the lands owned by the Palmer family of Fairfield, in Somerset, was at Worthing Library, but is now at WSRO with transcripts and derived maps of the farms.[5]

An eccentricity of fate has also preserved a set of manor rentals for a short period from 1602 to 1610. These say little about the size and layout of farms, but tell us about ownership and tenancy in those days. The originals are at Somerset Record Office, but copies have been transcribed.[6] Shortly afterwards, a steward's book for 1618 to 1621 recorded business at the manor court, and is invaluable, but needs translation from Latin.[7]

3 *Sea Road and Carnival, 1906, showing the Cricket Field entrance to the right, Jackmans Cottages gardens and the carnival parade, with the 'Queen of Hearts', Mr Lawrence, in top hat, and Louisa Villas family by the gate. The flint wall and pine trees adjoined Homestead farm.*

At WSRO there is a scheme to transcribe thousands of probate inventories. Between the 16th and 18th centuries, when a person died, a list of goods had to be compiled for probate purposes. Covering only moveable goods and crops, their great deficiency is in not identifying houses and lands, but they provide an invaluable picture of post-medieval domestic and farm life.[8]

Knitting these together are parish and school records, wills, deeds, rates, census returns and much else. There should be a wealth of material in the 'parish chest', such as poor relief from the late 16th century onwards, but the story is all too common, with most early documents lost by careless parochial officers.[9] It is only from the 1790s onwards that 'social services' leave some account, when local parishes 'united' as the East Preston Union and the first workhouse for paupers was built. The process may have been slow, but the vastly more humane social services of the early 21st century are the product of 400 years' growth and experience.[10]

It is not possible to note every reference from journals, chief of which is *Scribble*, a magazine edited by William Hollis, the developer of South Strand, from 1916 to 1919, or from local newspapers – *West Sussex Gazette* from 1856, and *Worthing Gazette* from 1883, a source that is far from exhausted.[11]

Notes

Land measure by statute measure

1 chain = 22 yards or 66 feet

1 acre = 22 yards by 220 yards

However, the traditional acre locally was about three-quarters of a statute acre, based on the amount that could anciently be ploughed in a day. Farm areas were reckoned in traditional acreages until the 18th century.

BL	British Library
PRO	Public Record Office
WSRO	West Sussex Record Office
SRO	Somerset Record Office
EPNS	English Place Name Society
SAC	Sussex Archaeological Collections
SRS	Sussex Record Society
VCH	Victoria County Histories
OS	Ordnance Survey [Maps]
WSG	*West Sussex Gazette*
WG	*Worthing Gazette*
WH	*Worthing Herald*
Rape	The Normans divided Sussex into several rapes, areas based on castles such as Arundel, to defend the seaboard and suppress the population.
Manor	A feudal estate managed by a manorial court, owned by the lord of the manor, in later times comprising copyhold and leasehold lands together with obligations from freehold tenants to pay quit rents and heriots.
Demesne	Land reserved to the lord of the manor as the demesne or manor farm.
Copyhold	Land held from the lord who owned the freehold, the title entered in court rolls or books, for the life of the tenant or more usually three of the family, or by inheritance.[12]

Freehold tenure	Freehold not held by the lord, but paying heriot and quit rent.
Leasehold	The lord's own manor farm was usually the first to be made leasehold, either year to year or for a number of years. At a later date, when copyholds, and copyholds for lives in particular, had to be renewed they were made leasehold instead.
Heriots and Fines	At a tenant's decease his best beast or a sum of money was levied and paid to the manor owner, the new tenant also paying a monetary fee or fine.
Quit rent	Payment by tenants to replace ancient customary services to the owner of the manor.
Terrier	A survey of land in written form.[13]
Glebe	Freehold land to support the parish priest.
Open field	Medieval arable lands were divided into large fields with acre selions or strips distributed amongst the tenants. These were cultivated in common and in surveys and maps were often called Commons – not to be confused with common pastureland, such as village greens.
Reeve	Elected by tenants of the manor to supervise the daily business and work.
Tithes	A tithe or tenth of the produce from farms. In Ferring Prebend – Ferring, Kingston and East Preston – the Great Tithe of corn or its value went to the Prebendary, or his lessee, the Small Tithe of other crops to the Vicar, and supposedly the Curates of East Preston and Kingston. The Prebendary, or leaseholders from him of the great tithe, was responsible for upkeep of the chancels of the three churches, leaving the naves to the parishioners.[14]
Prebendary	A Chichester Cathedral canon, in charge of its administration.[15]
Dates	The old style calendar was used until 1752, with 25 March as New Year's Day. Dates given in this history are as accurate as the available sources, or quoted.

1

DOMESDAY AND BEFORE[1]

With Rome withdrawing from Britain in 410 the province was left to its own devices for defence, and there were many Romano-British families who must have followed the legions into Gaul. Saxons and others were allowed, or could not be prevented from settling in parts of what became Sussex, particularly in the Ouse-Cuckmere region and in an area centred on Highdown.

The Anglo-Saxon Chronicle may be as much mythology as fact, but about the middle of the fifth century there seems to have been a more aggressive incursion into Sussex, with Aelle subjugating those British people that remained. This took place in 477 according to the Chronicle, although this date may be a generation late by archaeological evidence. To the Saxons the British became 'Welsh', that is, foreigners in their own ancestral lands.

Celtic place-names barely exist in this county, and Latin elements are few enough, as a result of Saxon culture imposing itself over the next couple of centuries, with villages acquiring Saxon identities. There is a continuing debate about place-names, over whether some 'ham' village names are earlier than 'ing' names such as Angmering.

The Arun estuary extended across to Angmering, providing its outlet to the sea, and there may have been salt marsh compartments along a long-lost shoreline.[2] Between the river floodplains fertile brickearth had long been settled and farmed, with abandoned Roman villas occupying select sites.[3] North of the Downs a wooded Weald was used for pasturage, with coastal settlements connected by droveways, which continued in use for another thousand years. Many of these inland pastures still belonged to coastal parishes in the 19th century.

By the early seventh century Sussex had been extensively settled with villages, both Ferring and Angmering being named after family groups. Other names speak of royal ownership, as with Kingston. But if Preston existed, its original name is lost, the present name indicating ownership by priests, presumably Christian.

Sussex was the last Saxon kingdom to be fully converted to Christianity, when St Wilfrid – erstwhile Bishop of York – came on his mission in 681, being aided by several 'miracles'. The Church soon made its influence felt, with vast lands given to it and to monastic foundations. Some charters of the eighth century are suspect, including grants of land at Ferring about 765 and 792 to a church which presumably already existed.[4] But East Preston and Kingston were not connected to Ferring until *c*.1150, when Bishop Hylary created Ferring Prebend and associated the parishes under one vicar.

A pagan Saxon cemetery on Highdown has been excavated, although no associated settlement has been discovered. The region this commanded included the estuary of the Arun, and the coastal plain to the east. This area became the administrative district called Risberg Hundred, renamed Poling Hundred by 1296. Risberg may derive from the OE for 'brush covered hill', which immediately suggests Highdown, the geographical centre of the hundred. As the site of the first Saxon settlement, this vicinity is a contender for meetings of the hundred court.

Numerous manors evolved within Risberg royal estate, which extended from Burpham to Goring, Nunminster forming a large part, incorporating Rustington, West Preston and Poling. But before the Norman Conquest, only Lyminster remained in the king's hands, although this was far larger than the modern parish, according to Domesday Book of 1086, with Clapham included in a group of settlements. Kingston is hidden in Domesday, and it is only in the 12th century that it emerges, together with Wick near Littlehampton, as manors given to Tewkesbury Abbey. It is a reasonable assumption that Wick and the 'king's farm' had both formerly been part of that vast Lyminster estate.

By the time of Domesday Book, virtually all of Sussex had been transferred into the hands of Norman families. East Preston was in the occupation of an obscure Robert, probably the Sheriff of Arundel who died in 1087. But its Saxon owner had been a woman named Wulfeva, and the interest here is that her major possession was Hamsey in eastern Sussex, with East Preston one of two outliers of that place, all held directly from King Edward.[5]

Robert holds Preston from the Earl. Wulfeva a free woman held it before 1066.
Then and now it answered for 7 hides. 14 villagers and 1 cottager with 4 ploughs.
3 salt pans at 30d. Value £4

Another feature is that no land is described as 'in lordship', which implies that the villagers occupied all of the seven hides of land, with no manor farm set aside by Wulfeva or Robert. Although a hide is notionally 120 acres, there is the complication that the traditional local acre was about three-quarters of a statute acre. In any case the seven hides were a taxable extent, and not an exactly surveyed area.

Another matter of interest is the three salt pans. The only other pans locally were at adjoining Nunminster and Lyminster, whereas a tidal Arun might be expected to have had more. The intriguing possibility

4   Church spire from Burnt House croft and barn, c.1925.
St Mary's Church spire, former Rustington Parish Cottages, and Burnt House Barn (to the left).

arises, that the Lyminster pans were in fact at its outlier of Kingston. Therefore all the local salt works would have been grouped together on salt marshes adjoining the mouth of the Arun. A large area of marsh certainly existed south of Rustington into the late 16th century.[6]

In Norman times modern parishes were in process of formation, and there is no certainty that a church existed at East Preston, although Domesday Book did not list all churches. However, the site of the churchyard is peculiar, adjoining West Preston, and it may have served both places.

2

LORDS OF THE MANOR

After Saxon thanes were unceremoniously deprived of their lands by the conquering Normans, in 1066, such people as Wulfeva disappeared into obscurity. In her place, under a new king, baronial overlords took possession of Sussex, with Earl Roger acquiring the western rapes, East Preston being amongst those manors that passed eventually into the lands of the Duchy of Cornwall but after 1540 reverted back to the earls of Arundel. However, the manor was not in their personal estates, but held from them firstly by Robert of Goring, and then successively by the Milliers, Tregoz, Palmer and Colebrooke families. These were the true owners.

Humphrey de Milliers, steward to the Earl of Arundel, was the first of that family to own the manor, by 1165.[1] The succession after that was involved, but in the 13th century part of their lands extended across into West Preston, before being split off into the hands of others of the Milliers family. It is of significance that until the 18th century East Preston was also called Preston Millers. It is probable that this family built both the present church, and established a manor house farm after links to West Preston were severed.

After the decease of Humphrey Milliers in 1241, his sister apparently granted the manor to John Mansel, who claimed to be Prebendary of Ferring.[2] As a councillor of Henry III, John fled to France in 1263 and died there, and the manor was temporarily taken over by Simon de Montfort the younger. Various conflicting claims were at last resolved when it was sold to Henry de Tregoz of Goring in 1271 for 250 marks which is £166 13s. 4d.

The family of Tregoz took its name from Troisgots in Normandy, with various branches holding lands in this country.[3] At times during the 14th century Preston was settled on a Tregoz son or widow, and it may be supposed that the manor house would have been occupied by members of their families. Last of the line John Tregoz died in 1404 and later his widow, so that by 1428 a cousin, Sir Thomas Lewkenor, inherited the lands. That family continued in ownership until 1526, when Edward of Kingston Buci – Kingston by Sea at Shoreham – sold it for £500 to Robert Palmer of London, one of a new wealthy merchant class.[4]

Meanwhile Kingston, having been owned by Earl Roger in the 12th century, was given by the family with Wick to the refounded Abbey at Tewkesbury.[5] These were the only lands in Sussex to be owned by that great monastery.

Robert Palmer descended from Sussex ancestors, and his acquisition of East Preston manor provided the land ownership necessary for attaining social and political status. Little more may have come his way, but for the Dissolution of the Monasteries. This brought the major windfall of Parham and other Westminster Abbey lands, together with the Tewkesbury manors of Wick and Kingston in 1540, for a mere £1,255 and an annual rent to the crown of £6 12s. 4d.[6] Henceforth Kingston and East Preston were closely linked both through the church and now as manors. At the same time, the related Palmer family of Angmering were taking over the Sion manors there. When Robert died soon afterwards, in 1545, he was still described as a mercer of London.[7] It was his son, Thomas, who settled at Parham, building the present magnificent house there after 1577. At that time Catholics, the family were far from being alone in the faith amongst the gentry of Sussex, managing to survive a tumultuous century.

Indeed their fortune soon took a new course, when the Queen gave Sir Thomas wardship of Elizabeth Vernai, heiress to an estate in Somerset. Her marriage to his son William secured the Vernai lands for the family, although William died in 1586, only four years after his father.[8] His son, Sir Thomas, served under Drake and Hawkins in several campaigns in the period of the Spanish Armada, later having command of a ship in the capture of Cadiz. However, the uncertain situation in England on the ascent of James to the throne led Thomas to emigrate to Spain in 1605 where he immediately died of smallpox, after having sold Parham to Thomas Byshopp.[9]

As a result, the widow and young William moved to Fairfield in Somerset. He later rather chose a quiet studious life, living much of his time in London and dying in 1652 during the Cromwellian Commonwealth. The estate then passed to his younger brother Peregrine, who was of his grandfather's adventurous mien but an army officer, serving with the Royalists during the Civil War in several major battles.

After Peregrine passed away in 1684, the estates went in normal succession to Nathaniel and then Thomas and finally his brother Peregrine, who led sedate lives as gentlemen and MPs. So the family came to an end, with the residue of their lands passing to Arthur Acland, owner of Rustington. But the Sussex estate had already been sold by Thomas in 1722, the greater part going to the banker James Colebrooke, including East Preston and Kingston.[10]

James was born in the borough of Arundel, son of Thomas Colebrooke, a former mayor. By 1722 he was living at Chilham Castle in Kent, and was succeeded in 1752 by another James who lived to the year 1761, leaving a daughter Mary. A brother, George, was an MP for Arundel and is the main subject of the Tompkin Diaries, which have been published.[11] So it was that, in 1761, Mary Colebrooke both came of age and married John Aubrey of Bucks. The marriage settlement required the sale of the estates, and as a result Preston, in 1772, came temporarily into the hands of John Bagnall, while Kingston was acquired by John Shelley of Michelgrove.[12]

Kingston was virtually a single entity now, in the occupancy of the Olliver family, so that in 1786 they were able to purchase it entirely.[13] On the other hand East Preston was in a number of tenancies, with much of it freehold, so that in 1773 it was dispersed into several hands, with the manor farm, the only substantial remnant of the old manor, purchased by John Corney of Littlehampton, later of renown for the Corney Charity, which still exists.[14] Kingston was now a closed parish, its village barely surviving. Its neighbour was neither owned by one lord nor even by the village itself. By 1743 manor courts were no longer mentioned at Kingston, but the manor house at East Preston had to provide for these until the end of the century.[15]

5   The Lido at South Strand, c.1938.
This shows the sea wall protecting South Strand from the sea where the beach was cut back in Kingston. The Lido was built in 1924 and is now the site of a house behind a restaurant. Angmering Court Club is to the right.

3

COASTAL EROSION AND POPULATION

At the end of the last ice age the Greater Seine had present-day Sussex rivers amongst its tributaries. Rising oceans filled this valley and created the English Channel, so that some 4,000 years ago the sea was only a few feet lower than today. A coastal plain of alluvium and brickearth had formed below the chalk Downs before the Ice Age, covering a raised beach which runs below Highdown through Angmering and Goring.[1] This plain was one of the most fertile farming areas in the country, and in the early 19th century wheat yields were still in excess of most other places.

We may never know to what extent the Saxons found the Highdown area abandoned by the British when they took control in the fifth century, but it would have been absurd for them not to have adapted the settled landscape and farms to their own use and ways. Evidence for Romano-British field patterns has been found in the district, with Saxon fields imposed on them, and where major boundaries existed between estates, these would not have been altered with impunity.[2]

The coastline was not only much further south, but different in character. To some extent the mainland was fronted by pasture and salt marshes until the 16th century, no doubt protected by shingle bars and beach. As the sea rose these were finally inundated, after which coastal villages suffered an erratic erosion of their southern common fields through the next three centuries.[3]

East Preston at Domesday was perhaps one of few compact manors locally, and its seven hides of brickearth farmland, with a 120-acre hide, would make the manor very approximately 630 acres in extent. The common fields may have reached 27 chains south of the present beach, with about 165 acres more land than today, and salt marsh to the south.

According to the Randall Map of Ferring, by the early 17th century the sea had encroached over half that distance, with Kingston Chapel falling under the waves by 1640.[4] In 1671 there was only about a chain more land than in the 1759 estate map, which has a coastline varying around three chains south of the present beach. There is little reason to

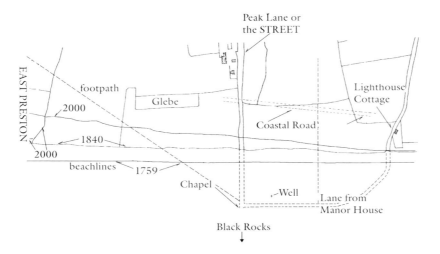

6 *Map of the Kingston Chapel area, 1630.* *Generalised reconstruction using evidence from the 1635 glebe terrier. Coastline shown at various dates, with the modern Coastal Road located. A well base was excavated in 1981, and the lane junction with Kingston Street was probably just south of the well. Black Rocks are twice the distance of the well from the headland.*

think any particular great storm caused vast loss of land during the latter period.[5] A remarkable alignment of fields in local parishes suggests an earlier convex coastline centred on the boundary between East Preston and Kingston.

Nevertheless, these inroads were not gradual but occurred during heavy weather, and any loss of protective beach would result in chunks of some poor cottager's farm being eaten up by the sea. The last clear example occurred over several years from 1912 up to and after the great storm of January 1918. Some six acres of land was lost, directly east of South Strand, and the cause is not hard to find. South Strand developers, particularly Mr Hollis, had so improved sea defences to the estate that he congratulated himself on the amount of shingle built up, using it to construct roads. Longshore drift had been interrupted and a small stretch of Kingston became exposed to the gale's full force.[6] At Littlehampton, though, the Arun was breached and the town suffered disastrous floods.

Returning to the early days, with an economy based on farming village population was fixed within limits according to the productivity of the area remaining unconsumed by the sea. Even allowing for a few independent families working the salt pans, to add to the 15 households in Domesday Book, the village had under one hundred inhabitants at the time, and Kingston was probably of similar proportions.[7]

The manor survey of 1321 provides evidence that the village had increased to above 150 souls, with several freemen families and 26 servile, and other returns give evidence for Kingston being of similar size. But the bubble was ready to burst. The Black Death of 1348 came after half a century of bad harvests and famine in England. It accelerated a collapse of the feudal system.

By the early years of the 17th century Kingston still had its village by the sea, but with under 20 households, as calculated from a 1626 petition for the demolition of the chapel.[8] East Preston was more safely situated but, a few years later in 1641, no more populous, although plague may have taken its toll.[9]

Seventeenth-century parish registers record births and deaths with tolerable accuracy, and crisis years are starkly portrayed, with long-term effects on population levels calculable. It is evident that local villages would normally have had burgeoning populations but for migration to towns, where death rates were higher. With village farms descending from father to eldest son, younger sons often had no recourse but to migrate.

The crisis years in Sussex are well enough known, such as 1609 with its heavy plague mortality in places like Chichester, and again in 1639, although these isolated crises were soon overcome. But the worst years overall were from the late 1660s until 1679 when village populations could only have reduced. Rustington in 1670 had four times the number of deaths to births, and in 1679 Ferring had rather worse figures. This was when London suffered its worst known plague and fire.

Generally most deaths occurred in the winter, but a deteriorating climate with harvest failures in the 17th century tipped the balance. More recently the blacksmith's wife recalled how, in January 1881, a snowstorm set drifts against Forge Cottage that blocked the ground floor, so that bread had to be delivered through the bedroom window, and a funeral could not take place.[10]

So it was that, in 1724, a survey estimated East Preston as having 20 families, or households,[11] rather more houses than recorded in contemporary manor surveys. At this point villages were about as small as they had been since the Black Death, but from this base the modern population explosion began. Improving agriculture could supply the rapidly expanding commercial and industrial centres. Local villages provided the people that moved into these towns, and surplus grain to feed them, before the American prairies were opened up.

A century later, in 1801, East Preston still had only 20 village families, the one great difference being the acquisition of the union workhouse. Agriculture at this time was certainly 'extensive' but could not have been very intensive due to the minimal amount of labour available. It took till the end of the century for the village to grow to 50 households, or more than double in size, excluding the workhouse and coastguards. Kingston was now diminutive, with two main households and a few cottages.

But village society and its economy were still integrated, and remained so until the second decade of the 20th century, when South Strand garden village and Kingston Gorse were being developed. From that point forward an increasing section of the parish was only casually related to the village,

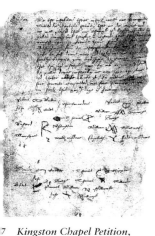

7   *Kingston Chapel Petition, 1626*
In January 1627, by the modern calendar, the householders signed this petition for the chapel to be demolished, so as to save the timbers and stonework: 'yt ys licke to fall downe very suddenly'.

8   *Forge Cottage, c.1905. Albert Booker and son, the blacksmiths, are standing next to the forge. Preston Place park is on the opposite side of the Street.*

and many indeed merely had second homes here. The population soared beyond 1,000 people and by the outbreak of the Second World War more than 2,000 people. With its new estate, Kingston expanded to 300 souls. Old constraints on population no longer applied.

Estimates for extent of coastline south of present-day beach

1086	27 chains maximum	1321	18 chains	1626	8 chains
1671	4 chains	1727	3 chains	1838	1 chain

1898   approximately as present day apart from a wedge of land at the west end of Kingston mainly lost early in the 20th century

Population in East Preston and Kingston

1641	85	*	*	K ...
1801	170	*	*	K 53
1911	773	*	*	K 62
1931	1333	*	*	K 160

1991   5338 including people in the addition to parish south of the railway in 1985.

In 1801 nearly half the East Preston population were workhouse inmates; in 1931 about four hundred.

9   *South Strand, c.1910. Tamarisks, where Mr Hollis first stayed in East Preston, Kingmere, and Salona, the earliest houses at South Strand, with a brick kiln in the distance.*

4

MEDIEVAL FARMS

There is only one substantial record of life in East Preston before the transformation in society that took place in the 14th century, precipitated by the Black Death. In 1321 a survey, or Extent, was made of the manors owned by Sir Thomas Tregoz, and what it portrays is so far removed from post-feudal society that it is difficult to visualise.[1] A picture is painted of long-established servile customs, binding villagers to an endless routine of exacting duties to the lord of the manor, tending his demesne farm. In return they were allowed the tenancy of smallholdings barely enough to maintain a subsistence for their families. When not working together on the manor farm they were working their own strips in the common fields, and all under the supervision of the reeve.

We can only imagine the catastrophe of plague in 1348, reducing population so that movement to a monetary economy was hastened. The

10 *Harvesters loading a wagon.*
A harvest scene probably near Pigeonhouse Lane.

11   *East Preston Manor House, 19th century.*
This is the appearance of the farmhouse that replaced the medieval building, before Admiral Warren enlarged it in 1913. It had knapped flint walls with brickwork, and a tiled roof.

villagers became copyholders, paying rent for their lands instead of service to the lord, while the manor farm was let out to professional husbandmen who employed day-wage workers from an increasing proportion of landless villagers and others with inadequate holdings. On the Downs, where agriculture was much more marginal, villages were already decaying and Barpham, on the downs above Angmering, was gradually abandoned, its church finally falling out of use in the 16th century.

The populations of Kingston and East Preston were much the same in number, although only a third of that of the nearby townlet of Angmering, with its several manors, but in all places the common field economy would have been similar.

The manor was called Preston Milleres from its previous owners; indeed, one of the two freemen on the jury of villagers helping to make the survey was a William de Millers, the other being William de Preston. Unfortunately the freehold lands were not described, although it is clear that they were concentrated in the east of the village, as in later years.

Tregoz was only concerned about the extent of his own lands, which by very fine, but not necessarily very accurate, measure totalled just under 200 statute acres, and perhaps another 100 acres of pasture for 150 sheep. If only all the fields had been related one to another, it would be possible to reconstruct the geography of the village, but, as it is, only the general picture can be deduced.

The Manor House with its three acres of garden and orchard, and pigeon house nearby, was where it would ever be, the present-day Midholme site at the north end of Sea Lane. Surrounding it was the most valuable corn land in the manor, and amongst the most valuable in all the manors owned by Tregoz. To the south may have been much of the pasture, while most of the villagers' lands lay in common fields down the centre strip of the village, between the main roads, through the Street Furlong to the South Common. The South Common is now under the sea. One particular field called Lathemere can be identified with modern Lashmar (Road) Field north of the school. It is the oldest surviving place-name we have.

It may not be entire coincidence that the fields fall into three lots of 23 acres, and possibly three more at 40 acres, suggesting how a three-course rotation of wheat, barley, to beans and a short fallow may have been organised. In terms of the traditional local acre, which was how the furlong strips were generally estimated, this translates as two 120-acre hides.

Twenty-six families were accounted for as working this land, in exchange for their diminutive 'farms'. Eleven principal tenancies were of six acres, with 16 others ranging from four acres down to small crofts – one family had two of these holdings. For the major smallholders, rent was 9d. an acre, together with work on the manor farm that would have taken up to 57 days to complete. The lesser tenants had evidently commuted their services for rental payments, averaging as much as 2s. an acre. In comparison, at nearby Ferring, owned by the Bishop of Chichester, villagers had larger farms and could in theory be required to work every day of the year on the manor farm, except holy days. They were fortunate if they had families to work their own lands.

12 Hay making at East Kingston, early 20th century.
A scene on the J.A.S. Candy farm at East Kingston which was the original Kingston Manor House.

The work demanded was described in the utmost detail. Ralph le Hunte, for his six acres, owed 4s. 6d. rent each year. His duties included reaping over 10 acres of corn, for which he was paid at 5d. an acre, threshing four bushels of wheat (a day's work) hay making, awning barley, washing sheep, carrying sheep hurdles, spreading dung, and making malt. The peculiar exactness of 10½ acres, 7 acres and 5¼ acres, for the land to be reaped by various tenants, again suggests a conversion from old measures using the local acre. Villagers and their families no doubt worked together on these stints, where possible.

William Opilhude is an example of tenure at high rent with few duties:

> 1 messuage and 2 acres of land and owes for rent of assize 4s. 4d. namely on St Thomas's Day 2s. 2d. and at Midsummer 2s. 2d. and he owes 1 hen on St Thomas's Day and he owes 4 boonworks in harvest at the lords food and he must furnish one man to help make and collect 4 acres of hay.

By the 15th century this work on the manor farm would have been commuted to monetary rents, and a figure of 1s. 3d. an acre may have been fair, and is indeed typical of the copyhold rents that were charged in the 17th century. It is also notable that the total area of land these villagers occupied, at 105 acres, was similar to the later extent of copyhold land.

There is no indication of free land in Domesday Book, but that situation changed rapidly, presumably as a result of transactions by the

13   *Threshing corn at Baytrees Barn, c.1910. Threshing corn with a steam-powered thresher. The barn was built at a time when hand threshing with a flail was still the rule.*

Millers before the mid-13th century. There is one instance in 1201 when it was recorded that William de Millers gave land to Jowet de Preston, of at least 50 acres.[2] It may be assumed it was one of her descendants who was on the 1321 jury, serving the village after which they were named. Their holdings were later comprised in such farms as the Homestead, Beehives, and House on the Bend.

Apart from a few wealthier villagers, and the manor house itself, the ordinary villein would have had insubstantial dwellings that did not last. But a survey of church lands in 1635 lists 36 garden plots, called hollybreads, paying tithes to the vicar, a large proportion of which would once have had houses.[3] Most of these were, as may be expected, along the Street and present-day Sea Road, and maybe North Lane, as the only known lanes in the village until recent times, but a few were lost 'in the sea' as a result of recent coastal erosion. Apart from the main village a small hamlet to the south can be envisaged, and tenuous support for this is provided by the 1201 transaction, which mentions a western road down to an obscure 'hospice' by the sea.

These common fields and their management by the villagers had virtually been extinguished by the 17th century, with enclosure by agreement creating a manor and parish of privately controlled holdings. Improved agriculture and profits masked the inestimable loss of a link between community and property. All the servile customs of the medieval village were reduced to a few obligations and privileges by 1671. For East Preston:

> Every freehold tenement payes releife and herriott the best beast after the death of the tenant dying seized and after every alienation
> All estrayes and felons goods and wreck of sea doe belong to the Lord of the Mannor by prescription[4]
> That the coppyholders (on every death or surrender) doe pay for each coppyhold tenement herriott the best beast
> That the widdow of each coppyholder shall have her bench ... paying but a penny fyne to the Lord and the Stewards fee
> That the coppyhold tenants shall have (by lycence from the Lord or his Steward) tymber for repaires if any be growing on the tenement
> That if a coppyholder doe suffer his buildings to be ruinous and fall it is a forfeiture
> That every copyholder may by lycence from the Lord demise his copyhold for seaven yeares hee paying for the said lycence a yeares Lord's rent
> That the copyhold tenant who was last admitted shall be Cryer at the Lord's court and have for his fee jd on every admittance
> That a copyholder may surrender out of court into the hands of two customary tenants of this mannor to be presented the next court
> That after the death of a customary tenant his heire shall be admitted before another paying a penny lesse fine.

For Kingston in 1671 the customs still needed to consider common field usage:

> That the freehold tenants doe pay releife, suit of court, and other customary services
>
> That the customary tenants on every death or surrender doe pay for each coppyhold tenement herriott the best beast
>
> That the widdow of a customary tenant either for life or of an estate of inheritance shall have her husband's estate dureing her bench ... paying noe fyne to the Lord, and the Steward's fee
>
> That all the coppyhold tenants are to have tymber (by licence from the Lord or his Steward) for repayres if any be growing on the tenement
>
> That if a copyholder cutt tymber without licence or doe fell any or suffer his buildings to be ruinous and fall hee shall forfeit his tenement
>
> That the right of inheritance doth discend to the oldest sonne and if there be noe sonne then to the eldest daughter and if there be neither sonne nor daughter then to the next of the kindred who is heir according to the course of the comon law first to the male then to the eldest female
>
> That on the admittance of an heire two years value of the land shall be sett for a fyne and one year on a surrender
>
> That the heire of a customary tenant for life shall be admitted to fine before any other and pay a penny lesse therefore
>
> That a surrender may be made of customary lands into the hands of the Lord by the acceptance of two tenants to be presented the next court
>
> That if the heire of a coppyholder of estate of inheritance after the death of the ancestor come not in and clayme before three proclamations passe at three courts it is a forfeiture of his coppyhold estate unlesse such heire be beyond the sea or in prison or under age, and then they think the Lord may take the proffitts untill such heire appear after the third court past
>
> That the youngest (viz) the tenant who was last admitted shall be Cryer of the Court and have for his fee on every admittance 1d
>
> That if a customary tenant shall demise his copyhold land without licence from the Lord or his Steward for more than a yeare and a day 'tis a forfeiture of such estate and that for such licence hee shall pay for every yeare the same is granted xijd [12d.]
>
> That all tenants of this mannor as well tenants of the Lord's demesne lands as freeholders and customary tenants that have land in the common fields may for every tenn acres (after harvest till the same shall bee plough'd and sow'd againe) put in seaven rother pole beasts one yearling and one wayner and for every acre two sheepe.[5]

MANORS AND RENTS

Not until a mere 400 years ago did the two villages emerge from the shadows into a fitful light of history, with places and people that can be identified. Both manors were now owned by the Palmer family of Parham, and later of Fairfield.

In 1602, besides the great manor farms, and a demesne windmill at Kingston, there were still a dozen copyholds at Preston and 14 in Kingston, although it only had three small and one large freehold farm. On the other hand East Preston boasted seven freeholds of various sizes, paying quit rents, besides several small farms entirely free, such as those owned by the manor of Ham. It is notable that the large Beehive freehold in fact comprised three ancient holdings, so the Palmer steward was paid a heriot of an ox for each one when Thomas Greene died.[1]

The remarkable feature is that the majority of households in each village had at least a few acres of land. In 1626 there were nine such households in Kingston and only eight purely labouring families.[2] Preston had around fifteen landholding families and, with a few tradesmen as well, plain labourers' households were in the minority.

14   *Beehive Cottages and farm buildings, c.1920. Beehive farmhouse when it was used as cottages. Behind it are the farm buildings, including stables and threshing barn, today comprising the Village Hall.*

In terms of basic rents collected in 1602, the Palmer lands in East Preston brought in £20 15s., of which £11 3s. was for the manor farm, and only £1 1s. for the freeholds. At Kingston the manor farm was worth rather more at £14 2s. and the windmill £4, with freeholds only 18s. 9d., in a total rental of about £32 10s. This hides the real situation, with additional income from fines and heriots when tenancies changed hands, but set against that various expenses in running the general Sussex estate with its stewards, rent collectors, and numerous allowances for repairs to copyholds. In a typical year the Sussex manors were worth under £500 after expenses, with Wick and Donnington the greater part of that.

But these rents were becoming outdated, and it was the leasehold rents that could most easily be increased. Kingston manor farm was the first, with a massive boost to £100 a year, although it was some time before Preston manor farm followed to a similar level of £75. This was in the order of 10s. an acre. Copyholds were much more difficult, and the device eventually used was to make legal 'agreements' changing copyholds, for terms of lives, to leaseholds. The change was masked by making the initial conditions similar to ancient customary copyholds, for a duration of three lives, and at the same old rent. So we find, in 1686, the new tenant of Rosery's 12 acres [Old Forge House], paying a massive £60 fine, for a lease of 99 years and three lives, at the old copyhold rent of 15s. Life was short in those days, and the term of years meant little.[3]

By 1671 there were three new leaseholds in East Preston for 21 years or more, with large farms created out of a number of copyholds. By the early 18th century the manor had five leasehold tenants, including the manor farm, with the rest freehold, while Kingston, although retaining copyholds of inheritance, nevertheless had the vast majority of these lands gathered into the hands of two members of the Olliver family. This family started on a route to monopolising Kingston when Thomas leased the manor farm in 1686. Then, as other farms fell vacant or were sold, and as the village decayed and fell into the sea, the easy course was adopted of selling to local wealth in the form of his family. The process was completed in 1786, when cousins William and George Olliver purchased the manor outright. In Preston no such monopolist asserted himself, and the Colebrooke lands fell into several hands in 1773.

At Kingston, it is notable that common field enclosure by 'agreement', fairly negotiated in the manor court, favoured the large farmer such as Olliver, allowing his strips to be gathered into large blocks. In 1691 the 13 strips at Northinghurst under several owners were exchanged with others belonging to William Olliver, so that he thereafter owned the entire field. A similar process took place in the south part of Mill Common, and a Lammas meadow where the pasture and hay was shared.[4] But equally remarkable is that even in the mid-18th century, when only the small May and Elphick farms remained independent, all the 'inclosed' lands were still reckoned as parts of the open fields, with the manor court presumably regulating their use.

Rentals of 1743-4 show how farms had increased in size and value.[5] In East Preston the manor farm was leased by Thomas Lulham at £98 annually. Thomas May was leaseholder of Baytree House and former Elphick land in Kingston at £98 13s. Charles Hills, for his blacksmith shop and the Rosery [Forge House], paid £12 and Oliver Penfold for Beehives farm £48, while, at Kingston, the manor farm and most of the other lands were held by William and then Thomas and George Olliver [d1786] at £222, rising to £270 in 1763, or over 13s. an acre.

Rents varied, but taking the manor farm at Preston, and its area as calculated in the 18th century of 162 acres, including a field in Wick, in 1602 it brought in under 17d. an acre, but then for a hundred years from about 1680 a more realistic figure of over 9s. an acre, rising to 12s. by 1742. In 1763, with extra land added, a £140 rent represented 16s. an acre. The Baytree farm, however, was already near £1 an acre. The most significant change was that the total rent value of East Preston and Kingston was almost as much as the whole Palmer estate in 1602, vastly outpacing general price inflation.

With improved farming methods, and the French wars at the end of the century bringing inflation, rents doubled, compensated for by a great increase in wheat prices. Therefore farms cashed in by ploughing up most of their fields. At Kingston the brooks could only be pasture, and the fields by the sea remained so, but to the north over thirty acres in the Old Lands pasture, and Park meadow, became arable. East Preston manor farm also had three-fifths of its hay meadow and pasture in the village, 78 acres, reduced to less than 15 acres.

The manors had therefore now become quite nominal, and associated with that came the demise of agricultural management in common by the village, but with the unlamented loss of common fields in their countless small strips. Kingston now contained just two private farms, the social effect of which was made more pronounced by local government being based on parish and property. East Preston remained a more open village retaining a vestige of parochial democracy.

In the early 19th century, George Olliver father and son (d.1861) owned west Kingston, with its new house now called Kingston Manor, while their relation Samuel Henty and son had east Kingston. George Olliver extended into East Preston with his acquisition of the Homestead in 1812, and his relative William Olliver obtained Corner House in 1819, building Preston Place there later.

East Preston manor house was owned and occupied by the Corney family, but with part of the old farm now in the hands of John Slater of Preston Cottage. Nearby, Baytree House farm was acquired by Gratwicke of Ham about 1823. Much of what had been the Beehive and the House on the Bend formed a new farm owned by another external magnate in the form of George Henty of Ferring. Finally, the small Baytree Cottage holding was held by Richard Baker, the last yeoman farmer in the village. Where land was leased to tenant farmers rent at around £2 an acre could be obtained.

These ancient farms were now having fields exchanged to create more compact holdings. But this itself was a temporary prelude to a process of amalgamation similar to that which had already occurred in Kingston. Reginald Augustus Warren married into the Olliver family in 1850, taking up residence at Preston Place, and for the next fifty years barely relinquished an opportunity to purchase lands that came onto the market in the village.[6] But for the rise of the horticultural industry, and other trades, this Olliver-Warren clan might have held almost all the village householders in thrall, in tied farm cottages.

However, by the end of R.A. Warren's life in 1911 farming had become less profitable because of cheap imports from abroad, and other easier profits could be had on this Sussex Riviera. Within a generation most of his land had been sold for residential development, so the face of the village and its social structure changed entirely.

15   *Window detail at East Preston Manor House.*
This detail shows the excellent knapped and squared flintwork around one of the original windows of the east front.

16   *Preston Place and Beagles, c.1905.*
Preston Place south side facing the gardens and park, with its ironwork conservatory. The Wooddale Beagles with, probably, Mr Warren on the left in the dark coat.

PRIESTS, THEIR HOUSES AND FARMS

The modern parish was formed about the time that Norman manors became defined, and was largely based on them. Saxon minster churches had served far larger territories, and Ferring was probably the mother church of Kingston, but whether East Preston came under Ferring or another minster is not clear. It is possible that the churchyard was a burial ground for both East and West Preston. The Millers family, who gave their name to the village, established a manor farm and presumably built the church on this burial ground during the 12th century. There is as yet no evidence for any preceding Saxon church on the site. The date at which Kingston Chapel was built is lost to the sea and history. It may not have been coincidental that the Prebend of Ferring was instituted by Bishop Hylary of Chichester in the mid-12th century.[1] East Preston and Kingston were thereafter associated with Ferring under its vicar, apart from briefly during the Commonwealth.[2] This continued until 1913 when the Vicarage of East Preston with Kingston was created.

Large parishes often had chapels of ease in outlying parts, but Ferring Prebend was three parishes, with Preston and Kingston claiming to be free chapels, the lords of the two manors having the patronage or right to appoint the curates or chaplains.[3] Certainly most ecclesiastical administration, and also civil administration as it evolved from the 16th century onwards, was quite independent in each parish under the control of elected churchwardens and other officers. Glebe farms in each of the parishes were occupied by the curates, who also had houses provided for them. In 1584 a jury of aged villagers, recalling the situation before the break with Rome, suggested that the vicar had taken over the glebe and tithes illegally:

> Kingston was ever a Free Chappell and did belong to the Abbatt … and he did alwaies appoynt a Curate there and the seid Curate had the land there … And had a mancion house wherein he alwaies dwelled … Preston is a parishe churche … and the Curate did dwell in the saied parishe and did lett the seid land … and the Lord of the seid manor did alwaies appoiynte the Curate.[4]

Previously, in 1579, Steven Foules served as curate at East Preston, when his house was 'impayred and discovered in some part'.[5] A curate was living at Kingston in 1590, although where is not known. Unfortunately all trace of these dwellings seems to have gone by 1635, when the glebe terrier would otherwise have mentioned them. It is conjecture that the Preston house was located at a small glebe croft in North Lane near what is now Roundstone Drive. By that date the vicar of Ferring had taken over all of the glebe for himself, together with small tithes paid by farmers out of their crops, and all claim to separate patronage had been abandoned.

Coastal erosion had an unquantified effect on the extent of glebe in each parish, with medieval areas quite unknown. In 1584 estimates were that Kingston had five customary acres and Preston 16 acres, say four and 12 acres statute measure. Kingston also had a half-acre in Wick, which is surprising until it is recalled that both places had been owned by Tewkesbury.[6] By 1635 the areas had reduced to two-and-a-half acres in Kingston, including a small plot next to the doomed chapel, and 13¾ acres at East Preston, including an acre at Hearne and a quarter acre in the South Common, both soon lost into the sea.

All that remained in Kingston was the two-acre plot west of what is today Peak Lane. In Preston a substantial area survived, comprising a notional three acres south of the church, eight acres at Roundstone together with another small plot, and an acre strip between Sea Road and Sea Lane. Almost all of the East Preston glebe was sold to Messrs Warren in 1912, leaving a reserved plot south of the churchyard.[7]

From the 17th century onwards, curates were often employed by the vicar, but it was not until 1863 that a curate specifically for East Preston once more appeared in an expanding village, the recently created Ecclesiastical Commission providing a grant for this purpose. From then

17 *Roundstone, before 1914.*
The house north of Roundstone Crossing, as it was when Rev. Williams was in occupation. Its appearance is much the same today.

until 1913 Roundstone House, by the railway crossing, was rented for them. In that year the separation of the parishes was accomplished, and a new vicarage of East Preston with Kingston was created, the reserved glebe plot used for building the vicarage house. The Rev. Trevor Williams, who had been curate, was instituted by the bishop in November.[8]

Estimates for the value of the living from all sources in 1656 were £50 for Ferring with Kingston, and £20 for East Preston, which remained unchanged through to 1724.[9] By 1851 Ferring was said to be worth £194 and Preston £62, including glebe at £60 and £20. At that time the curate received £40 from the vicar, but in 1863 the Ecclesiastical Commission guaranteed £100. On separation of the parishes in 1913 the new vicar of East Preston was allocated £163 plus another £45 as workhouse chaplain, very similar to the vicar of Ferring at £223, which was average enough for parish clergy.[10]

Curates designated for East Preston at Roundstone House

1864-67	Frank Ley Bazeley BA	
1867-69	H.R. Morres	
1869	Gregory Bateman MA	
1869-71	Charles William Palin MA	
1871	Henry Fulham Which MA	
1872-84	Samuel Sharpe Walker MA	(buried at Preston 1894)
1884-6	Robert Henry Tripp BA	
1887-8	Edward Rawley Morris	
1889-1900	William Ridgly Nightingale MA	
1900-5	Frederick William Booty MA	
1905-8	James Louis Crosland	(also Vicar of Rustington 1908-41)
1908-13	Ernest Trevor Williams MA	

Vicars of East Preston with Kingston[11]

1913-35	Ernest Trevor Williams MA	(buried at East Preston[12])
1936-69	Frank Goldsworth Fincham	(resigned, buried at East Preston 1991)

18   *Church and cottages, c.1905.*
East Preston church has a 15th-century tower and stone spire. Rustington Parish Cottages are now demolished and the site a green. The parish boundary is along the churchyard wall. Vicarage Lane did not then exist.

CHURCH AND CHURCHYARD

Kingston Chapel was 'eaten up by the sea' in the 1630s. Very little is now known about the building, or even its patron saint. With the manor owned by Tewkesbury Abbey from the 12th century a chapel of similar date is likely. A simple flint rubble nave and chancel under a Horsham slab roof, with masonry windows, similar to East Preston, can be envisaged. After the Dissolution of the Monasteries, and religious turmoil of the 16th century, it shared the fortune of most churches by falling into decay. In 1573, 'Our chauncell is in great ruyne and decay and lyke to fall downe in Mr Shelleys fault of Lewes.'[1] Mr Shelley of Lewes had become leaseholder of the great tithe and so responsible for chancel repairs. Then, in 1602, came the only report on the church as a whole, before it was lost. 'The whole Chappell is unpaved the seats are ruinos the covring [of the roof] greatly decayed the glasse windowes and doores neede mending the walles whiting they allso want a bible a pulpitt and linnen clothes for the communion table.'[2]

The first literary reference to the village is in the 1623 poem *The Sussex Constable*, by John Taylor, where the chapel must have been a landmark to all seafarers close by the shore:

> A plowman (for us) found our Oares againe,
> Within a field well fil'd with Barley Graine,
> Then madly, gladly, out to sea we thrust,
> 'Gainst windes and stormes, and many churlish Gust,
> By Kingston Chappelle and by Rushington,
> By Little-Hampton and by Middleton.

Finally, came the forlorn pleas in 1626:

> Our chappell is much decayed and out of repayre by reason of the sea, and now hath wrought away the land in a manner to the very chappell so that it is not repayrable. And being allotted to the mother church of Ferring, we most humbly desire order may be granted unto us to take downe the covringe and healing of the chappell, which is of very good and large Horsham stone or slate and enable the parryshioners for the preserving of the stone and timber worke for the yearly and

continuall benefitt of the poore, for suddenly the chappell will be ruinated by the sea.[3]

In 1641 the last churchwardens' presentment for Kingston confirms, 'Our Chappell is utterly ruinated and demolished by the sea, and wee doe constantly resort to Ferring to service being the mother church.'[4] No doubt the chapel was south of the village towards Black Rocks, but these massive natural conglomerates were simply used as markers to describe where the building lay, much nearer to our present shoreline.

Whether the church of St Mary the Virgin existed at East Preston before the 12th century is unknown, but by the 13th century the existing building had acquired its present form.[5] A Norman nave with a chancel of *c*.1200 formed one continuous space, without a dividing arch as is more commonly found, although a timber rood screen at the junction is a virtual certainty, removed after the Anglican church became Protestant. The principal feature of the chancel is still the triple lancet east window, with its dividing shafts of Purbeck marble and stiff-leaf capitals – traces of a similar window can be seen at Ferring. Under its lofty sill would have been the high altar with an ornate reredos, dedicated to All Hallows. From 16th-century wills it is also known that an image of the Virgin Mary stood in the church.

Each side of the nave there were round-arched Norman doors, of which only the north door survives. But the nave was almost devoid of windows, with small lancets mostly in the north wall, perhaps unglazed and closed by shutters. Such light as there was played on walls ablaze with colour, portraying biblical stories and mythology. In the 15th century more ornate windows were installed, having pairs of trefoil-headed lights, which would have been glazed. One of these is in the nave and two in the chancel.

An 18th-century drawing shows the ruins of a small lean-to building on the south side of the nave, with stone walls and a Horsham slab roof. It has been spoken of as a possible anchorite's or hermit's cell, for they were not uncommon in medieval England; one unlikely alternative is an ossuary for bones removed from the churchyard.

The manor passed from Tregoz to the Lewkenor family in the 15th century, at which time the present west tower was erected with its spire, elegant window and internal archway. The church was unique in western Sussex in having a stone spire, made of Quarr from the Isle of Wight, until it was sadly removed in 1951.[6] It may be supposed that the tower was built to house the three bells, which survived until the 18th century. The remaining tenor is one of the ancient bells of Sussex, cast by widow Johanna Hille between 1440 and 1443, at almost 30 inches diameter and over five cwt.[7] A strip of land near present Somerset Road was called Bell Acre, its rent used for church and bell maintenance. This land belonged to the parish rather than the church itself, and was not sold until 1936.[8]

Unfortunately the mid-16th-century English Reformation brought considerable destruction of art, in the act of suppressing imagery, ceremonial and superstition in parish churches. Subsequently, the word as the basis of truth helped usher in the Enlightenment reading of the universe.

As with Kingston Chapel, decay was much in evidence in the 17th century, and in 1602, 'The glaswindowes and pavinge of the Chappel neede mendinge and the covringe of the Chappel and porch the north doore and the stoone worke over that and the south dore have neede to be repaired the stoneworke of the steeple.'[9] But these were fault-finding exercises and much that was good had no mention. Not that funds for repairs were unavailable. In 1637 the churchwarden had to pursue a claim in court for non-payment of a church rate by the manor farm tenant. A matter of 3d. per acre was no mean amount in that era.[10]

However, 18th-century reports indicate generations of complacency. In 1724, 'The Church … in good repair excepting the plate on the north wall which is broken and has been oddly supported by a prop these twenty years. They say the ivy is so necessary and eradicable that the roof cannot stand without it.'[11] It was not until 1791 that new blood in the parish got to work:

> The Parish Church has been in a most ruinous and dangerous condition for many years past. Two of the main Beams having been long broken and Propt up … there must be taken down at least Forty feet of the Roof several of the Rafters being found broken … there are Three Bells the frames of Two of them become so very weak and rotten so as not to be rung without imminent danger … if sold would greatly contribute towards the necessary Repairs … We deem one Bell sufficient for calling the Congregation together.[12]

A faculty was granted[13] and some £119 was expended on a new roof, using nearly £46 from the sale of the two smaller bells. This is not the

19   *Black Rocks, 1981.*
This group of large conglomerate rocks may be approached at neap tides, due south of Peak Lane in Kingston. They are the traditional but probably quite false location for the lost Kingston Chapel.

present roof but one at a lower level continuous with the old chancel roof.[14]

Over the next seventy years other small changes cumulated, so that several more windows were placed in the nave, and the old timber porch was replaced in 1842 by the present flint-walled enclosed porch.[15] A tower porch was removed later, perhaps in the course of 1863 tower repairs.

Then in 1868-9 came the great rebuilding, with more space required for an expanding parish, most notably by the inmates of a large new workhouse. Around £1,500 in subscriptions was expended, principally on building the south aisle, but requiring yet another nave roof at higher eaves level.[16] It also seems evident that the chancel roof was replaced. In 1908 Mr R.A. Warren referred to the use of drawings by Sir Gilbert Scott, but perhaps that great architect was not directly involved. Even so, in 1893, summer visitors and workhouse inmates made accommodation tight, until modern times.[17] The Early English style chosen suited the Low Church convictions of the parish.

One great contemporary disaster overtook the church, with the removal of the spire in 1951.[18] It was known in 1938 that restoration was urgent, but intervening war years prevented action in time. Stone from the spire can still be seen facing a chimney-breast at the south end of Baytree Cottage. The spire had been an inspirational landmark above the trees to all who walked through the meadows from the village. Since then the church has sunk into obscurity, with Vicarage Lane built up and extended about 1967.

A church room had long been needed and was eventually provided and dedicated in 1982, as the Spire Room, making use of a fund intended for spire rebuilding. An excellent concept, it was like an octagonal chapter house, avoiding interference with the excellent external flintwork of the south aisle. But soon afterwards better access and facilities were needed, and in 1999 plans were considered for a radical extension off the nave to the south.

20   *Edwardian bathers.*
A beach scene near the Coastguard Boathouse, at the end of Sea Road.

**21   *Church and cottages
with lychgate, after 1913.***
*Station Road corner
soon after the lychgate in
memory of R.A. Warren
had been erected. On the
right are former Rustington
Parish Cottages, and in
the centre Burnt House
Cottages, demolished for
the modern roadway.*

The burial ground, originally one customary acre, extended only a
short distance south and east of the church until a southern extension
was dedicated in 1901, and others to the east in 1938 and 1962, doubling
its size.[19] Flint walls to the west side mark both the churchyard and parish
boundary. On the other side were Rustington Parish Cottages, flint walled
and thatched, the south part single-storey, extending from a probably
much older hipped cottage and acquired by Rustington parish after the
1722 Poor Law legislation. They were demolished for road widening,
and in 1937 the site was given to East Preston church, the residue now
being a green.[20]

For most of its history the burial ground was like a meadow with
graves only briefly marked. In 1579, 'Our Vicar doth sometimes put both
oxen and kyne into the churchyard'.[21] Not until the late 17th century
were gravestones used, and only one of that century survives, near the
chancel wall. All the earliest headstones are located north and east of
the church, a few being moved when the Spire Room was built in 1982.
They are distinctive in style, and it will be a great loss when they decay
away, some of them having pithy epitaphs that would never be permitted
today. 'Stay Pasanger behold and see. As you be now so Once were wee.
As wee are now so must you be.'[22]

The Church – 200 years illustrated

The following drawings and photographs cover two centuries of the parish church from 1791 and the last images of a medieval church, to the present inheritance of Victorian gothic.

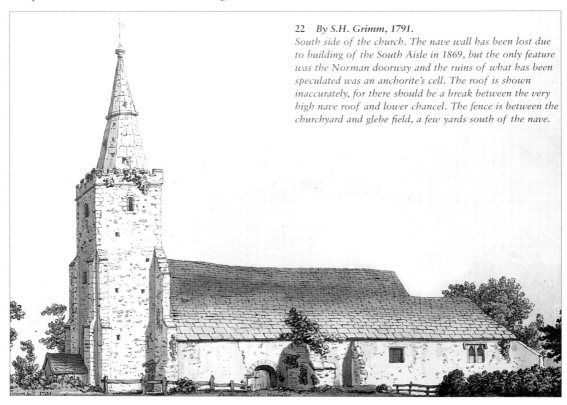

22   By S.H. Grimm, 1791.
South side of the church. The nave wall has been lost due to building of the South Aisle in 1869, but the only feature was the Norman doorway and the ruins of what has been speculated was an anchorite's cell. The roof is shown inaccurately, for there should be a break between the very high nave roof and lower chancel. The fence is between the churchyard and glebe field, a few yards south of the nave.

23   By J. Lambert, 1791.
A view of the north main entrance and churchyard side. The tower porch was demolished in the 1860s. The timber north porch was replaced by the present porch in 1842. More windows were inserted in the nave after that date. This drawing is not entirely accurate for, although the chancel had a lower roof, the wall is unlikely to have been set back from the nave wall.

24   By L.E. Partridge, before 1841.
This excellent watercolour by an unknown artist is invaluable in portraying the church after the new roof was built in 1792, but before other 19th-century alterations and installation of more windows. The gate is to the vicar's glebe field. Note the workman in his smock. The general surroundings and tombstones appear to be fairly accurate.

25   By Borrer, 1851.
St Mary's Church, the east end and north side, viewed from Parsons Way stile. By this date the present porch and new windows had been installed. The triangle of stone in the tower wall is probably the line of the medieval roof.

26   Church with west porch, c.1860.
An Angmering cameraman took this earliest known photograph of the church. The north side had become much as we have it today, apart from the west porch, and the accuracy of the 1841 drawing is confirmed, with the roof at one level. The farm gate was necessary for access to the glebe field adjoining. Who was the character in a round frock - the sexton?

27   View from Burnt House barn, before 1913.
In 1869 the south aisle was built with another new roof, making the church much as it is today, minus the spire. Ornamental gates to the churchyard had been installed, but were replaced by the lychgate in 1912.

8

The Parish Government

In the past a country was defined by its religion, the moral code of which was the basis of law and social convention. Besides the magistrates and parish policeman, it was the Church, and the church in each parish with its priest and vestry officers, that exerted moral authority locally. Increasing religious toleration from the later 17th century, and the cult of the individual, has brought freedom from custom and convention.

There is no surviving record of parochial business prior to the Reformation and Elizabethan Settlement. It is only from a few wills that we find people were concerned about their souls, leaving funds for masses to be said: 'I will have a trentall of masses at my buryall.' Or about tithes tardily paid: 'I bequethe to the high awter … xijd for my tithis forgotten.' Similar donations were made to the 'power mens box' to relieve the poverty that overtook ordinary villagers in old age and sickness.[1]

How they coped with swings in religion and authority during the following years is not recorded. By the 17th century few people were openly Catholic, certainly not in 1641 on the eve of war, with only one local man in Angmering refusing the Protestation Oath. More than twenty men in East Preston signed, together with the curate, and all in Ferring with Kingston.[2]

During the reign of Elizabeth it became evident that legislation for poor relief was necessary and the 1601 Act created overseers of the poor, as vestry officers in charge of relief, with a compulsory parish rate. The two parishes are not alone in having lost these poor relief records. This system continued locally until 1791, when a workhouse for paupers was built in East Preston to serve a group of parishes.

At Kingston, depopulation by sea during the 17th century was made a virtue when the remaining landowners kept a 'closed parish', excluding and removing potential paupers, and poor children being sent away on cheap apprenticeships. Expenditure on the poor from the late 18th century onwards was only around £10 a year, with typically 4s. a week paid to a widow, but much greater expenditure arising when removal cases were taken to court. Kingston had no need to join the Union and use the workhouse until legislation required this in 1869.

In East Preston population remained stable, but by 1800 the inflationary effects of war and blockade caused expenditure to treble to around £270, in a population of no more than twenty households. It may be assumed that most wage earners were in receipt of poor relief, with some twenty children and seven adults placed in the workhouse. After the war years the parish kept to its normal allowance of around a couple of inmates, the others being on outdoor relief. In 1825, shortly before the Swing Riots, 22 were on permanent relief and a similar number temporary.[3] Peace, and British dominance of world trade, brought better conditions later in the century.

Gifts and charities were only encouraged on a formal basis for administration by the churchwardens and overseers. There are early 17th-century accounts of a 5s. charity from Robert Young and £5 left by Thomas Martin, and then in 1685 a 5s. annuity from a house in Arundel, and £5 left by Martin Chalke. However, it transpires that in 1613 Thomas Martin of Angmering had left £5 to the poor of East Preston, but in 1676, 'Marten Chalke was Churchwarden and Tho. Baker paid in the £5 given by one Tho. Marten of Angmering to Marten Chalke aforesaid Churchwarden.' The £5 was merely handed on to churchwarden Chalke, and his will has no bequest. The 5s. and £5 funds were lost after 1800, when the substantial Corney Dole came into operation.[4]

That bequest by John Corney, in 1805, was made when a bread dole might have kept some people out of the workhouse.[5] Interest, originally of £13 16s. a year, was to be distributed on St Thomas' Day, 21 December, half in bread and half in money. The tablet recording this is still over the church door. Since 1894 the charity has been a Parish Council responsibility. In 1911 it was reorganised by the Charity Commission, at which time a large number of people were receiving useful amounts in goods, but inflation has now reduced the value of some £30 in income.[6]

> John Corney Yeoman late of Little Hampton by his Will in the Year 1805 gave to the Poor of East Preston £15 0s. 0d. which deducting legacy duty is £13 16s. 0d. yearly for ever to be distributed on the 21st day of December half in Bread and half in Money.

By 1911 ancient customs of parish and union relief were giving way to national welfare. In 1908 the five-shilling pension was introduced, and a few grandparents of today's villagers were grateful beneficiaries.[7]

All substantial villagers were expected to take part in governance of the parish. Churchwardens were not so much elected as rotated by property, and half of them signed

28   Corney Charity tablet over the north door, which was to be 'kept legible' but is barely that 100 years later.

29 *The chancel, c.1910. An invaluable picture of the chancel when it conformed more to Protestant belief, and the High Church of the Rev. Williams had yet to transform the interior. The only stained glass is the Olliver memorial windows on each side. A small communion table is flanked by the Ten Commandments. There is certainly no rood beam. There is an eagle lectern, although even then the pulpit was to the side and not central.*

by marks up to the 18th century.[8] So it was with other unpaid officers: constable, waywarden looking after highway maintenance, overseer of the poor, and clerk, although the last had to be literate.

Responsibility for the church is illustrated by a churchwarden's presentment of 1662 when almost all the landowners were reported for not having repaired their sections of the churchyard fence.[9] The parish was also required to pay for upkeep of the nave – made good use of for church ales and parochial business – from church rates, although the rector or prebendary had care of the chancel.[10]

As civil authorities dealt with more heinous crimes, the Church was left to deal with carnal excess, and absence from Sunday service and instruction. Adultery and its consequences could undermine social order. 'John Wythear and Alice Payne have had a chylde in adulterie.' Then, later in the 16th century, 'William Oulder and Alice Hatcher he supposed to have begot her with child and neither of them have doon penaunce.' John Gray in Kingston was a notable reprobate in the 1620s. 'We present John Gray for not dulie repayring to church upon Sundayes and holidayes ... for living after an ungodly and wicked fashion in shameful usage of his wife beating her ... for drunckenes and resort to alehouses.' In 1625 he was reported as having been excommunicated.[11]

In East Preston several presentments were made for men working on Sundays, although it is clear that a farming village could barely avoid it. 'We present Richard Whittington for grinding corn many Sabbath days. We present William Upperton of Preston for going with his wayne and

30   *The chancel, early 20th century, with 1919 pulpit, rood beam, a large altar, the Commandments removed, and stained glass in memory of a former curate. Today the altar table is set forward centrally in the chancel.*

his man William Bocket upon the Sabbath day carrying of corne.' And even worse, 'We present Thomas Millard for selling of ale and keeping of ill order upon the Sabbath days.'[12]

Churchwardens cast a censorious eye over not only the parishioners, but also their priests. Numerous questions in presentments had to be answered about the clergy. Perhaps the most serious allegations were those made in 1584 (see p.23) concerning tithes and patronage.[13] A century later, after the enthusiasm of previous years had died down, the ministry had become exceedingly relaxed. Eventually, in 1678[14] and again in 1692, the wardens complained bitterly that the vicar 'hath been Parson of Ferring about Twenty years and that he hath not come to the Chappellry of Eastpreston above once a fortnight at the most' and had even missed feast days there.[15] Little changed before the evangelical revival of the 19th century although, when a curate was available, catechism for the young at least, and visiting the sick, were duties attended to.

A distinctly Low Church opinion prevailed, with a pulpit dominating the chancel, four tablets of the Ten Commandments on the wall each side of a small altar or communion table, a minimum of ritual, and an absence of symbols such as the rood, in a whitewashed building.[16] Good Friday and Christmas were the only feast days observed. Religious and social conformity in the young was boosted, after 1840, by a Protestant Church of England village day school, and an associated Sunday school that continued well into the 20th century.

Not until 1865 was the Protestant calm broken, and then by its own kind: 'A very respectable Weslyan Preacher preaches occasionally in a cottage and sometimes in the open air.' But there was only a handful of Dissenters in the parish. Then, in 1898, a temporary dissatisfaction with the religious and moral state of the parish crept in: 'The opening of the brickfield is bringing a very low class of people in to an otherwise respectable village.'[17] By this time summer visitors were being spoken of, and a decade later the whole character of the village began to change with the building of South Strand.

Conflict came after 1913, when the Rev. Williams became the first vicar of East Preston with Kingston, a convert of the High-Church Oxford Movement. This brought him into conflict with members of the Parochial Church Council, who considered Roman Catholicism a sin, with the rood amongst items particularly opposed.[18]

A Free Church and Sunday services were established at the YMCA hut from its building in 1920, and when it was sold in 1967 the church moved to the nearby rifle range building until it was taken over for the Village Hall in 1981 as the Warren Room. As the 20th century advanced, greater religious diversity came to the village. Roman Catholics had to go to Angmering initially, but eventually they acquired their own church in Vermont Drive – Our Lady Star of the Sea – in 1957.

It was the separation of the civil and ecclesiastical parish in 1894, and the creation of the Parochial Church Council and church roll in 1920, that virtually disestablished the Church.[19]

31 Beehive Cottages and The Homestead, early 20th century.
View from Coke Lane (Vermont Drive) towards the Homestead farm, with its barn against the Sea Road, Beehive Cottages and barns centre, and Cricket Field with its flagstaff to the right.

9

FARMHOUSES AND FARMING LIFE

Farming with a little inshore fishing constituted virtually the whole economy in both villages until the 19th century. Cottage shops selling a few trifles of haberdashery and grocery came and went, anything more depending on the passing hawker or the market in Angmering and, more particularly, the weekly markets and several fairs at Arundel. Littlehampton did not begin to grow above village status until the 18th century.

A medieval commonfield landscape was gradually being transformed through the 15th to 17th centuries. Those holdings that were not freehold were moving through copyhold for lives to leasehold for terms of years, and all would eventually be sold off piecemeal, the manor ceasing to be meaningful in property terms.

It is impossible to locate, or in any way identify, all the farmsteads and cottages that existed in the post-medieval period. Even in the 17th century only a general identification of the lands in various holdings is possible. It is known from the Hearth Tax of 1670 that some 25 households existed in East Preston, but a general decline in population reduced this to about twenty households in 1724.[1] A similar decline in Kingston was partly occasioned by the sea destroying most of the village, so that by 1671 only some nine or so houses remained. But the principal farms benefited by this, in accruing multiple holdings, and these 18th-century farms can readily be identified, with the benefit of the Colebrooke estate map.

In 18th-century East Preston leaseholds comprised the Manor Farm and, now added to that, Bay Tree House nearby, Forge Cottage, Wistaria and the Rosery or Forge House. Freeholds consisted of the Homestead, Baytree Cottage, Beehives, House on the Bend, Old Yews and Corner House, and various cottages, at least 16 houses in all. For Kingston all that remained was the leasehold Manor Farm in East Kingston and holdings of mixed copyhold and freeholds based on the new West Kingston House, and four houses in the Street or Peak Lane.

At the top end of the scale with a nominal 170 acres was East Preston Manor House and the two principal Kingston farms. Other large

32 *Description of East Preston Manor House, 1671.*

'The Mannor or Farme House is Built with Stone situate (together with two Barnes a Stall and other buildings and the orchards Gardens and yards thereto belonging) … near the high way leading to the Sea …'

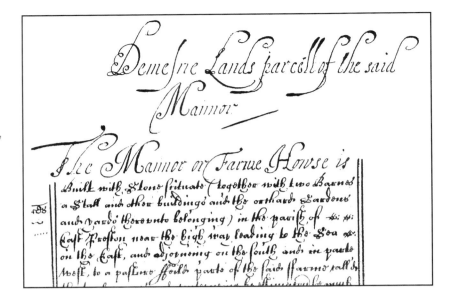

holdings were centred on Bay Tree House, Corner House, Homestead, Beehives and House on Bend, with the remaining farmsteads holding as little as eight acres, as at Baytree Cottage. This does, however, overlook the fact that a working husbandman might have land sublet to him by other owners, such as widows and retired men.

All the known farmhouses probably originated as timber-framed hall buildings, evolving to two full floors with brick chimneys and fireplaces by the 17th century, flint and brick replacing external framing under fully hipped thatched roofs, to produce the familiar Sussex cottages. The common layout inside was much as Baytree Cottage, a large central hall open to the roof, private rooms at the 'high end' where the master had his dining table, and service rooms at the other end. True cottages for the landless labourer are gone and forgotten.

33 *Manor House, c.1915, as extended south by Admiral Warren in 1913. The new flintwork is lighter in shade.*

34 *Sheep shearing at West Preston, early 20th century. A rather staged display of sheep shearing at West Preston, with Mr Bushby to the right and his shepherd left.*

East Preston Manor House (leasehold)

The 1524 subsidy or tax has William Mathew as the wealthiest villager, and in 1526, when the manor was purchased by Robert Palmer, the same William is given as tenant of at least part of the demesne.[2] No other early occupier of the farm is known.

In 1602 the farm was probably much as in later years, although perhaps not the fields. The demesne was then in two parts, the major leasehold held by Richard Parker, at an annual rent of £8 10s., and a small farm held by Edward Gawen at 53s. 4d. Possibly Edward had the detached Lashmar Field. From a 1637 court case it is known the farm was 'eight score and ten acres' which included a field in Angmering Park, all occupied by Nicholas Withers.[3]

From 1670 it was held by Richard Sotcher on a nine-year lease, at the greatly increased rent of £70 rising to £75. 'The Mannor or Farme Howse is Built with Stone situate (together with two Barnes a Stall and other buildings and the orchard Gardens and yards thereunto belonging) …' In other words, it was by then flint built as today, although any earlier structure has been lost in the present double-range house.[4] Beyond the orchards were the arable and pasture fields, reaching from the sea to north of the church, all as described by the 1671 manor survey. After Sotcher died, William Edwards took over in 1683 on an 11-year lease.

Various probate inventories provide a picture of the house and its contents, that of Edwards in 1691 being a good example (see Appendix 1). Although the exact form is unknown, the house consisted of four bays, a parlour, hall, kitchen and brewhouse, with bedchambers over, but the milkhouse and buttery probably in an outshut behind. By the 18th century a bakehouse is also listed with the service rooms. There were between one and three feather beds in every chamber (whereas poorer people might have had flock) with curtains and valences indicating that they were four-posters. A variety of other furniture included chairs, trunks and cupboards, with quantities of linen, and later such refinements as looking glasses, window curtains, a clock and pictures in the best rooms.

The parlour at one end of the house had little more than a table, a round table as a refinement, and chairs. Coffee cups made an entrance in the 18th century. The hall was one of the main rooms, with a table and forms for general dining. Besides dressers and cupboards, other miscellaneous articles were kept there, such as a still for making spirits, spinning wheels, and some of the crockery, with Delftware mentioned in later inventories. Next to the hall was the kitchen. Here the cooking equipment included iron jacks, pothooks, gridirons and spits, pewter dishes, plates and porringers, brass skillets and kettles, and perhaps a brass furnace used in brewing.

In the brewhouse were the brewing vats, churns, tubs, and all manner of utensils kept there for convenience. The milkhouse had its butter and cheese, moulds, crocks, weights and scales, a powdering tub for salting meat, and other random items. A buttery was the place where the beer butts were kept, although not always. Beer vessels, bottles, a brass boiling pot, frying pans, crocks of grease and other items found their way there. In the bakehouse, searches or sieves and baking troughs were mentioned.

The farm was not locally typical, with pasture predominant, other farms having arable dominant. Although a four-course rotation of crops

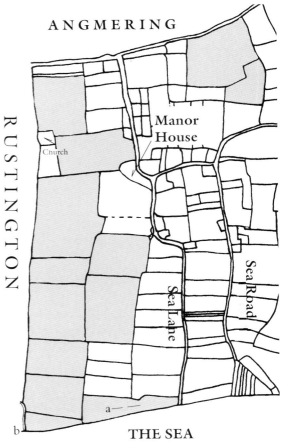

35   *East Preston Manor Farm, 1671.*
The manor farm remained in this area until after 1800. Road names are modern.
a – line of beach today.
b – line of beach on 1759 map.

was introduced by the 19th century, a long tradition of three courses was still in evidence, with wheat, barley and oats, and legumes. The first small mention of clover is made in the early 18th century, and root crops such as turnips are not in evidence until the 19th century.

The cultivation of some 160 acres of land required one or two wagons, a couple of dungpots or carts, several harrows and rollers, together with all the minor tools. In the early days a team of oxen was certainly used for ploughing, but later on horses were also used in numbers.

Livestock typically included about a hundred sheep of all ages, on extensive pastures, half as many cattle for fattening, and milch cows, with a smaller number of pigs. No doubt there were also chicken and geese but these were barely noticed in the inventories. Since the Southdown sheep had not been developed at this time, the older breeds must be assumed. These kept the arable lands fertile as well as providing meat and wool.

A working farmer with very little monetary capital had most of his wealth tied up in farm stock, some £200 to £300. To have over £60 worth of goods in the house was the mark of a substantial establishment.

Something of a family dynasty began early in the 18th century with John Hammond, who died in 1722. Thomas Lulham, who died in 1762, was a later member by marriage. In 1742 the farm was leased to him for 21 years at £98, after which George Wyatt took over at £140 for another 21 years, extending beyond the sale of East Preston.

John Corney of Littlehampton purchased the manor house in 1773 for £5,710, including the small Wistaria and Rosery (Forge House) holdings, and when he died in 1805 it was left to be shared by Corney relatives.[5] They gradually sold their interest, so that after 1844 the farm was split between Olliver, Holmes

HERE LYETH THE BODYE OF EDEN BAKER LATE WIFE OF IOHN BAKER OF EGLESDEN & DAVGHTER TO THOMAS TRVELOVE AND ALES HIS WIFE WHO FOR HER WISDOME VERTVE AND MODESTY THE LIKE HATH SELDOME BENE SENE SHE DECEASED THE XXVII DAY OF APRILL 1598 BEINGE OF YEAGE OF 23 YERE

36 *Eden Baker memorial.*
Brass in Angmering church for Eden Baker née Truelove of Corner House, 'Wife of John Baker ... daughter to Thomas Truelove ... her wisdome vertue and modesty the like hath seldome bene sene ...'

37   *Drawing of Preston Place, 1918.*
Watercolour of the east front of Preston Place signed 'P Seifert', a POW there. Note the iron-columned canopy to the entrance, and large shrub borders each side.

and Slater, but eventually the pieces fell into the capacious hands of R.A. Warren.[6]

Corner House (Preston Place) (freehold)

Corner House got its name because it stood on the corner of the Street and Worthing Road, until demolition in 1838, when Preston Place was built there. The property did not figure in the 1602 Rental, being a small freehold outside manorial ownership. It can be deduced that it was owned by Thomas Truelove at this time. It then passed to John Rose, who held two acres, the house and croft, which was evidently the only part of his farm in the village, other lands being in Angmering. Perhaps around the year 1640 more lands were acquired, creating a village farm of over 30 acres, as it remained for another 150 years. Thomas Truelove is also of interest because his daughter, Eden, married John Baker of Ecclesden Manor. She died in 1598 aged only 23, and a brass effigy and inscription may be seen on the chancel floor of Angmering church.

In the 1671 survey none of the farm is directly alluded to, and only incidentally is it noted as belonging to Oliver Weeks, a freeholder paying no quit rent to the lord of the manor. The names and location of its fields can be deduced, however, and are the same as in the estate map relating to *c.*1724, when it was owned by Elizabeth Hettly. Most of its land may have been acquired from the Homestead, although there is no firm evidence for this.

In the 1740s George Olliver (d.1786) was in occupation, when the property was owned by John Mounshire. He was probably joined by his young nephew William Olliver (d.1820) and mother, after she was widowed in 1745. William is reputed to have made some wealth for himself later, when he managed the George Duke estate in Littlehampton, marrying a daughter. It was his son William who purchased Corner House from William Elliott about 1819, and he died there in 1827, one of his sons demolishing the old house and building Preston Place in its stead.

Forge Cottage (copyhold)

Forge Cottage is still well known in the Street, although divested of its garden and forge, and no longer hipped and thatched but half-hipped and tiled. There is no reason to suppose it held the blacksmith forge until the 19th century, being a farmstead when tenanted by the Whittington family. John, in the late 16th century, followed by his widow Elizabeth, was copyholder in 1602 at a yearly rent of 22s.

In 1671 another John Whittington was the owner of the 23-acre farm, but the previous year it had been made leasehold for 99 years at the old rent. This was advantageous to the landlord, since as soon as the lease fell in it could be renegotiated at a greater rent, and indeed in 1684 the property was leased to James South and continued to be owned by the South family into the 18th century, until let to Thomas May of Baytree House at £12 rent.

The property was a victim of the 1773 manor sale, when William Henty acquired it, integrating the land into his Beehive Cottage holding. Thereafter the farmhouse was reduced to a cottage, of no great value to Beehive Farm. It passed into the hands of Gratwicke of Ham in the 19th century, aquiring a new life as a home for the village smithy, and the Booker family who lived there until 1957.

Wistaria Cottage (copyhold)

Wistaria Cottage is almost opposite Forge Cottage, in the Street, in appearance much as it was in the 19th century, a thatched flint-built small farmstead. Indeed, its old croft is still intact to the west, although now part of a recreation ground. The earliest known owners were the Masters family in the 16th century, Robert being copyholder in 1602 at six shillings' rent.

In 1671 Anne Masters held the 3½-acre smallholding as the widow of its former owner; in the customary term she had her 'widows bench', after which it was to go to her son Edward, who died in 1687. It then passed from the family to William Ingram, and in the 18th century was held by Elizabeth Ingram and son John Ingram, until he died in 1749. It had a similar fate to Forge Cottage, in losing its smallholding when it was absorbed into the Manor House farm in 1763 at £5 rent.

The Farley family were the next known occupants, several Charles in succession. One of these married into the Corney family, and farmed part of their large manor house estate. In the 19th century the house was simply known as Farley's Cottage.

Baytree House – Bay Trees (copyhold)

Baytree House is the large early 19th-century house north of the junction between the Street and Sea Lane; possibly the flint-walled north wing is earlier. Its farm had small beginnings, held by Robert Martyn in 1602 as a pair of copyholds at 26s. 8d. rent. His family had been in the village for at least the past hundred years, although it is not possible to say where they first lived. In 1656 yet another farm was taken up, the former Pocock copyhold of seven acres, at 14s. rent. As a result the Thomas Martin farm of 1671 was an estimated 31½ acres (although rather less by statute measure), but he seems also to have occupied another five-acre field which the survey omitted to mention. The farmhouse that had belonged to Pocock still existed but, as with so many other houses, disappeared thereafter.

38   Wistaria Cottage, c.1905.
View from cornfield across the Street to Wistaria Cottage, Forge Cottage, right, and Jasmin, centre.

39   Baytree farm buildings, c.1910.
'Bay Tree Corner East Preston', looking east, with the large threshing barn and smaller barns next to the house.

40 *Baytree House, 1997.*
A view of the house
during the carnival parade.
Originally the stuccoed
front was left unpainted.
The wing to right of the
chimney is modern.

Yet another great tranche of holdings became attached to the farm in the early 18th century, probably originating as four smallholding in 1602 which, when gathered together, became a farm known from its former owners as 'Hammonds, Ides and Bakers'. In 1656 Paul Laurence, a cleric who did not live in the village, took this up as a new leasehold, containing 34 acres at the greatly enhanced rent of £19. In 1686 it passed to William Baker for a 12-year term, and then at some date soon afterwards was acquired by Baytrees.

The occupier of the farm when estate map and other records were drawn up in the early 18th century was Thomas May, who had the lease of a fair-sized holding at about 70 acres by estimation and 57 acres statute, and also held old Elphick land in Kingston. Just before his widow died in 1750 the land was taken over by Daniel Simmonds, and their lease continued until 1773 when the farm was purchased by George Olliver (d.1786) who occupied Kingston Manor. Thirty years later, in 1802, his son sold it to George Cortis of Angmering, after which it passed through several other hands in rapid succession, with some small parts sold off, until in *c.*1822 W.G.K. Gratwicke of Ham came into possession.[7] After this the ancient Gratwicke of Ham lands in East Preston were added to the farm, so that now there were some 74 acres in the occupancy of his tenants.

Ancient Gratwicke lands consisted of two freeholds paying 1s. 8d. quit rent to the lord of the manor, and another set of fields paying no quit rent, in all about twenty statute acres.[8]

House on the Bend (freehold)

The House on the Bend was the only farmstead in Sea Lane until the 20th century, although there may have been associated cottages north of it at an early date. Part at least of the ancient house is contained within the present double-range building. Its farm was one of the principal freeholds in the village, owing a quit rent of 1s. 11d. to the owner of the manor. In 1620 it was estimated at 40 acres in traditional measure, and it is at least a possibility that this land, together with Beehives Farm, had all begun as a single estate of the Green family early in the 16th century.

In 1602 John Lenne of Wick was the tenant of Thomas Grene, although there is no knowledge of the terms of his lease. Thomas and his descendants continued as owners until 1737 and were often resident, although they also had lands in Rustington at various times. By 1671 Edward Green was in possession, but the quit rent had ceased to be paid and so the lands are not specified in the manor survey of that year and can only be traced in relation to other properties. The farm was clearly much the same as in later years, but by now the estimated area was only 32 acres.

When Thomas Green died in 1737 he was the last of the family and bequeathed the farm to his brother-in-law Edward Mearsh, pending the decease of another relative.[9] If a datestone on the property was removed from the house, as seems likely, then he had rebuilt it in 1723. The property then passed through several hands, eventually being put up for sale. In the event the land was broken up about 1791; two acres were purchased by the newly created Poor Law Union to build a workhouse, and William Henty bought the remainder to add to his Beehives Farm. This would have been the end of the story, but in about 1835 the house was acquired by William Amoore together with some fifty acres in the west of the parish as an independent farm once again. This only survived a few more years until 1865 when, inevitably, R.A. Warren of Preston Place purchased the property from John Batcock, to add to his burgeoning estate.[10]

41   *House on the Bend, 1980.*
The ancient farmhouse would not have had the bay window or porch, and may have been longer to the north, or left, with a hipped end that has gone.

Old Yews (freehold)

Old Yews was a house that recent generations will not have known, on the south-east corner of the junction between the Street and Sea Lane. It was demolished by R.A. Warren in 1876, and nothing replaced it, for reasons that are also lost. Although the house may have been early, it was unusual in being attached to the Homestead freehold property at the beginning of the 17th century, and only after 1635 did it become independent.

The house and land may well have been detached in 1642 at the same time as the Boxtree Cottage site. In the 1671 survey this property was of particular interest for its association with the brewing industry. It was accounted a messuage, malthouse, barn, and garden, with three crofts or fields totalling 12 acres, owned by William Holden of Ferring as a freehold paying 1s. 6d. quit rent. Who the maltster was occupying the house is not known but John Whittington, who died in 1651, was of that trade.

Later, in the 1720s and for another twenty years, William Richardson of East Preston was paying the quit rent as owner. But it is only after the arrival of John Slater in the village, shortly before 1751, that continuity

42   *Preston Cottage, 1901. Nothing is known of the appearance of Old Yews, although a traditional cottage is probable. Preston Cottage was built on another part of the farm, in a classical style but with vernacular materials, the fine-gauged flint pebbles which face the south front. The original door canopy is illustrated. George Corney, grandson of John Slater, is on the left with his family.*

in ownership can be traced. Three generations with his Christian name lived at the house, and it was the third John Slater who married Charlotte Corney, heiress to a share of the Manor Farm.[11] This last John, therefore, had other land, and so occupancy of the Yews was left to his mother and spinster sister Susanna when he built Preston Cottage. By this time the maltings had ceased to operate in the face of competition from local brewers such as Constable and Son.

Henry Slater was the last of the direct line, passing away in 1869, and his aunt Susanna shortly afterwards in 1872. The house with some of its land was purchased in 1874 by Mr Harding, the workhouse master, but he soon disposed of the house for £280 and in 1876 it was demolished.[12]

Rosery (Old Forge House) (copyhold)

The present house in the Street was until recently a restaurant. In 2005 it was extended, but much of the former house was built by the artist Heywood Hardy in 1909 and 1913. Only its central range is the 18th-century farmstead, and that itself was a new house replacing the earliest known dwelling on the site. It would seem to have been the Gawne family house and farm in the late 16th century, and in 1602 occupied by Joan Gawen or Gawne, the widow of Thomas, as a copyholder paying 15s. rent.

In 1619 the farm was estimated at 12 acres, which is what it remained for another hundred years and more. But the Gawne family were mortal and in 1644 several died as victims, it may be supposed, of the same typhus epidemic that was ravaging Arundel. Thereafter, in 1653, the copyhold was transferred to Thomas Lydgater until his decease in 1682.

Then there survives a unique document for East Preston from 1686, when the copyhold was given up and transformed to leasehold, initially in the name of William Woolvin, for several lives or for 99 years at the old 15s. rent, a fee or fine of £60 being paid by William for the privilege. The opportunity was taken to introduce into the lease[13] numerous regulations for good husbandry. Woolvin was still the tenant when the estate map was drawn up in the 18th century, his death occurring in 1730. The annual rent then rose to £12 when the farm was occupied by Charles Hills, blacksmith, but by 1763 it had become attached to the Manor Farm and leased to George Wyatt.

43   *Woollven headstone.*
'Here Lyeth the Body of William Woollven …' of the Rosery. These early headstones have a distinct character but are decaying fast.

44   Rosery, 19th century.
*Forge House today is a large building that hides the
original cottage named the Rosery. This illustration
reconstructs the appearance of the 18th-century house,
as it was until after 1900. A small central entrance hall,
with rooms each side, replaced an even earlier cottage
which would have had a large medieval hall.*

In the 1773 sale of manor lands, John
Corney acquired the Rosery together with the
Manor Farm, and its days as an independent
smallholding came to an end. By 1830 Elizabeth
Corney was living there, having opened it as a
beer shop for the village.

Winters (freehold)

No house name is recorded, but this would have
been so called after its owner's surname. It was
situated on the present Royal British Legion site,
hitherto the *Three Crowns Inn* built in 1872. In
fact the house was not mentioned in 1602 or in
the 1671 survey, since it had no farm attached
to it and paid no quit rent, and its presence is
only deduced from other sources. In the 1635
glebe terrier it was occupied by Stafford Wyse,
a blacksmith who died in 1643. It then passed
to Henry Brabey, another blacksmith with an
interesting inventory of his goods made at his
decease in 1695 (see below).

At last, in the 18th century it appears on
the estate map as a freehold owned by widow
Catherine Winter. She owned land in Angmering
and elsewhere so it should not be supposed that
this was a mere labourer's cottage. Her properties passed to Lucas and
other relatives in 1735. Then nothing more is known until 1791 when
deeds relating to the workhouse mention this neighbouring property as
being in the hands of Thomas Knight, and afterwards his widow Sarah
until 1857. The village beer shop, which had been at the Rosery, was
moved to Winters prior to 1851, and the *Three Crowns* was established
there in deed if not in name.

Amongst all the inventories of goods taken for deceased villagers
there is only one for a blacksmith. There are others for Angmering and
elsewhere locally, but the Brabey example probably has the best list of
tools and goods (nail – eight pounds in weight; shovel tree – handle;
weights and blades – balancing arm for weighing).

27.9.1695 £33 4s. 8d.
A true and perfect inventory of all and singuler the goods and chattells of
John Brabey late of Eastpreston in the parish of Ferring in the county of
Sussex blacksmith decd made taken and apprized the twenty seaventh day of
September in the yeare of our Lord Christ one thousand six hundred ninety
and five by Robert Tribe of Tarring in the said county blacksmith and Henry
Hoare of Burpham in the said county blacksmith as followeth (viz)

	£	s	d
Imp's his weareing apparell and money in purse	03	00	00
It Two pair of sheetes one table cloath and two towells	00	10	00
It One chest and one trunke	00	02	00
It Two tables, two joyned stooles and five chaires	00	05	00
It One furnace and one brass skillett	00	13	06
It Three pewter dishes and one saltsellar	00	05	00
It One pair of tongs and one pair of brandirons	00	02	00
It One firepann, one spitt and other small things	00	02	02
It One brass pott and five small beer vessells	00	12	00
It Two hoggs	01	04	00
It One hundred weight of new iron	01	00	00
It Nine nayle of iron tooles	01	04	00
It Four hundred weight and eleven nayle of old iron	03	07	00
It Two hammers, one sledge, one naile boll and three nayle of streake nayles and cloutes	00	19	00
It One beckhorne, vice, nayling hammer, block and tooles belonging to it	01	03	02
It The bellows, anvill, engine and fourteen shovel trees	02	05	06
It One new spitter, prong, waytes and blades	00	06	00
It Two pair of patten irons, fire pan bole and four pair of leathers for pattens	00	02	06
It Two pease hookes and two dozen of new shoes	00	08	06
It The cole trough, blocks, chestes, grinestone and trough	00	13	00
It Half a chauldron of coales	01	00	00
It Severall small debts due on books	13	00	04
It Desperate debts, old lumber and things unseen and forgotten	01	00	00
Sum total	33	04	08

45   *Boxtree Cottage, north side and east end, early 20th century.*
Boxtree was two cottages in the 19th century. The north front faced a garden and orchard and the east end was against Sea Road with a 1670 date in brick and flintwork, and H for Henry, I for Jane his wife, and M for Manning.

Boxtree Cottage (freehold)

Boxtree Cottage in Sea Road cannot be mistaken, with its 1670 foundation date in the gable end wall, although at that time it was probably half-hipped and thatched. Its garden originally included the shop site to the north. A medieval house may have existed here, being one of the garden plats listed in the 1635 glebe terrier, but in the early 17th century this was land belonging to the Homestead.[14] In 1642 it was purchased from Robert Lidford by Joseph Henshawe, who built the first known house, which must have been rebuilt in 1670 by Henry Manning whose initials form the datemark. As a small freehold with no farm attached, it was not mentioned in the 1671 survey. Nevertheless, Henry was a farmer who had perforce to lease land belonging to other people, and indeed he appears to have farmed the Laurence 34 acres.

After his decease in 1678 the house passed to relatives. Then, in 1697, it was acquired by William Baker, a substantial yeoman by local standards with tenancy of the former Laurence land. On his decease in 1713 the property went to others in the Baker clan of Baytree Cottage. But soon afterwards the house was divided into two dwellings occupied by Thomas Baker and Charles Hills, a blacksmith. The 1759 estate map has William Clear as the occupant, he having married Ann Baker. In 1795 it was sold and then in 1806 there began 120 years of ownership and

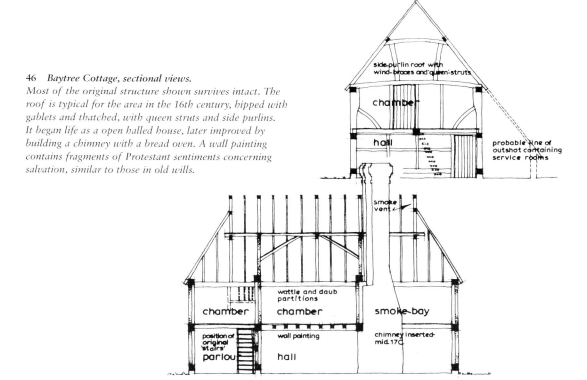

46   Baytree Cottage, sectional views.
Most of the original structure shown survives intact. The roof is typical for the area in the 16th century, hipped with gablets and thatched, with queen struts and side purlins. It began life as a open halled house, later improved by building a chimney with a bread oven. A wall painting contains fragments of Protestant sentiments concerning salvation, similar to those in old wills.

occupancy by the Ayling family. It was not until 1926 that the building once more reverted to being a single house.[15]

47   Baytree Cottage, c.1910, with Lorne Villa behind. At this date it was occupied by Mr Farmaner, a dairy farmer.

Baytree Cottage (freehold)

Baytree Cottage can still be found opposite the Conservative Hall in Sea Road, a timber-framed hall house of the mid-16th century, hipped and thatched, evolving to become a lobby entrance house, similar to Pendean at the Weald and Downland Museum, Singleton, near Chichester.

It is possible the Fuller family owned the house as far back as 1558, and were even its builders. Tenants included William Parker in 1602, although the rent he paid is unknown, but would have been far more than the nominal quit rent paid by Fuller to the lord of the manor of 1s. 4d. per annum. The land attached was presumably the eight acres of later years.

This farmstead has the remarkable record of a single family, Baker, owning it from 1630 to 1842 and in trust to 1869. Robert Baker originally came from Angmering to Kingston, where he was a churchwarden much involved when Kingston Chapel was destroyed by the sea in 1626. In East Preston the family also owned Boxtree Cottage for a time. Robert's will of 1643, by the modern calendar, is a good example of the Protestant form then in force, and is one of few that directly mention freehold land.

> In the name of God Amen I Robert Baker of East preston … being sike in body butt in good and perfect remembrance thanks be to god

48   Nelsons Cottage, early 20th century.
The Graperies house, amongst its greenhouses, with Mr Charman, the foreman until 1917, and his wife.

do make this my last will and testament ... first I resine my soull in to the hands of god the father and into the hands of Jesus Christ my redemer and my body to be buried in the Church yard of East preston aforesayd Item I give to the Cathedrall Church of Chichester fowre pence. [He then goes on to bequeath sums of money to several daughters.] All the rest of my goods and chattells and my free land in East preston I give to my sonn Thomas Baker ... I the sayd Robert Baker have set my hand and seall this eighteenth day of february 1642.[16]

The main farm croft comprised all the land currently occupied by the Martlets home in Sea Road. Other land adjoined North Lane, and later even part of Angmering.[17] In the 19th century another small area was acquired which later became the site of the Graperies Nursery in Sea Road.

In 1662 his son Thomas Baker died, and his probate inventory lists goods in various rooms, including the hall with its table on its separate frame, forms and joined stools, a lower chamber with feather beds, chests, and other furniture, a loft over the hall, with its bedsteads, an inner loft containing linen, another loft with a motley mixture of beds, wheat, barley, malt, a musket, and spinning wheels for linen and wool, a kitchen with all its iron goods, and brass, and a milkhouse with another medley including a salting trough and a furnace for brewing.

On the usual mixed farm were the following quaintly described tools and stock:

Item one wagen as shee gooes one dunckart as shee gooes one plowe two harrowes all other lumberment abroade ... Item three hoogs of bakne ... Item the light ioyrne ... Item thyrty fower sheepe & lames

49   North Lane Cottages, c.1910.
These cottages can be located today by reference to South Norris, the roof of which can be seen to the north. A range of shops was built behind this site. From right to left are Thomas Bennett and wife, Mrs Roberts of Elm Cottage, Charles Challen of the Three Crowns, *and then probably Louisa Barnett at her cottage, with others.*

... Item syx hoogs seven pigs ... Item fower cowes two twoyearlings
two twelvmonthings three wanyers two horse beasts ... Item thirteene
acres of wheat upon the growne ... Item nyne acres of barly ... Item
eight acres of teares & peas ... Item things unsenn & forgotn.

His entire goods and a little money were valued at £168 13s.

Exchanges of land after 1773 continued into the 19th century when
owned by Richard Baker, his smallholding increasing to over 10 statute
acres in the village, besides another four acres in Angmering. This was
mortgaged and the estate was placed in trust for sale after his decease
in 1842.[18] His widow later moved to North Lane Cottages, built by
Richard.

Beehives (freehold)

Beehives is a substantial timber-framed hall house of about 1500, with
a small two-storey cross wing at the south end. It is distinctive today
as a thatched and flint-walled pair of cottages next to the Village Hall,
which were its farm buildings, with the cricket field its croft. The gabled
north end of the building was a late extension, the original hipped roof
timbers hidden within.

The Green family who owned it in 1602 can be traced back to the
early 16th century, as notable landowners in the village, although exactly
where is unknown. Thomas Green of Upmarden would have had a tenant
farmer, in 1602, paying the 2s. 9d. quit rent at the manor court each
year, in addition to a much larger rent to Thomas. Shortly afterwards,
on the death of Thomas in 1607, three oxen were taken as heriots due
to the lord of the manor. Therefore his lands comprised three ancient
holdings, in all amounting to 80 notional acres.[19]

Prior to the 1671 survey the farm was occupied by Robert Brook,
who died in 1639. His rent of £6 13s. 4d., or nine marks, indicates the
value of good farmland at the time. Some time before 1671 the quit rent

*50 Beehive Cottages,
early 20th century.*
This farmhouse was briefly
three cottages, but since the
19th century has been two.
In origin a timber-framed
house, the north end was
just to the right of the
north door, with a hipped
roof.

ceased to be paid, and the property became an absolute freehold. The farm had passed out of the hands of Green of Upmarden to a Mr Evans, and was later owned by Francis Robatham of Middlesex. Then, in 1736, a peculiar reversal in status took place; James Colebrooke purchased the farm, bringing it back into the manor which he owned, but now leasing it out himself together with his other farms.[20] Typically, in 1742, it was let for 21 years to Oliver Penfold at £48 rent.

This only lasted until the general manor sale of 1773, after which William Henty became the owner. His was a notable family owning Church Farm, Tarring and being tenants of the Bishop of Chichester at Ferring Grange (the Tarring branch later emigrated to Australia with their sheep). In about 1791 the House on the Bend lands were also acquired.

Finally, in 1835, trustees for George Henty of Ferring sold this large combined estate in East Preston to George Olliver of West Kingston, and very soon Beehives was reduced to cottages.[21] What had been the bulk of its land was now attached to the Homestead.

51   *Homestead*, c.1910.
This shows the west, garden side, the east side facing directly into a barn yard with all its buildings and animals. During Mr Harding's occupancy the farmhouse retained much of its rustic character. Under a thatched roof timber-framed walls had been rebuilt in flint and brick. At the south end was the drawing room, next a dining room, then opposite the passage at the west entrance door a small morning or drawing room and, presumably, the staircase, with the kitchen at the north end. An outshut, or lean-to against the kitchen, by the west entrance, housed a flag-floored dairy with slate shelves, and in an outbuilding projecting eastwards from the kitchen was a scullery and stables. The dairy farm amounted to some 28 acres around the house.

Homestead (freehold)

The Homestead was the finest surviving timber-framed house in East Preston until it was demolished in about 1960, making way for the flats of the same name in Sea Road. The site also included two former cottages by the road about which little is recorded. This large farmstead had never been altered to cottages, or rebuilt in the way of other farmsteads in the village. It can only be assumed there had originally been the usual central hall, with service rooms at the north end and parlour the other end. Its history before 1600 is unknown but in the early 17th century it was owned by Edward Reed of Ewhurst at 9s. 7d. quit rent, his tenant farmer John Young also being an owner of property in the locality according to his 1611 will.[22]

Eighteen years later the central freehold was reckoned at 60 acres, known later as Windsor Farm or Winders. But it can be deduced that three properties were owned, with 1s. 6d. rent representing 12 acres later separated off and attached to Old Yews. Another 2s. 1d. was rent for land as yet unidentified, but quite likely fields later acquired by the Corner House. Windsor itself, therefore, had a quit rent of 6s.

Evidently Reed then sold the property to Robert Lidford. An involved business, with lands relinquished and other lands acquired, followed, the main transaction taking place in 1648 when Robert Lidford of East Preston sold Windsor Farm to John Cook of Goring for £500. The Cook family are notable in Goring, with memorials to them in the church.

By 1671 two more tenancies had been acquired by John Cook: Parker's freehold of eight acres that in 1602 belonged to Richard Threele of Loxwood, at 2s. 1d. quit rent, and a former eight-acre copyhold of William Parker, at 10s. rent, called Kerns. The copyhold had been made leasehold for 99 years in 1671. A total of 77 acres was now reckoned for the whole farm.

The Homestead remained in family hands until 1706 when it was sold to a merchant called John Deane of Arundel, for £873. It then passed to his daughter, Elizabeth, and she is given as the owner in the Colebrooke map of the manor, prior to her marriage in 1735. There are some errors on this map: Kerns is listed as freehold in the explanatory legend; in fact Kerns was not purchased outright until 1773. The family with its relatives did not dispose of the land until 1805, when James Goble of Burpham conveyed

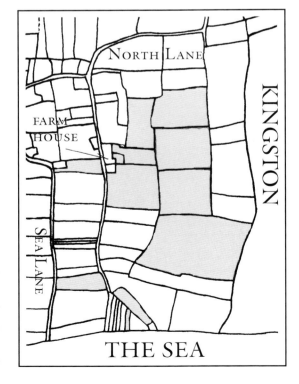

52   *Homestead Farm, 1671.*
The main Winders or Windsor part of the farm with some of the outlying fields. Road names are modern.

53   Homestead east side, 19th century.
An accurate representation of the east, garden front, of the farmhouse in the late 19th century.

the farm to James Penfold of Goring for £3,750. James Goble is one of five Sussex men who served on HMS *Victory* that same fateful year.

With East Preston manor fragmented, a general reordering of fields took place about 1806, so as to make more compact holdings. The Homestead gave up several fields to Baytree House in return for a block of land adjoining the farmstead, although the greatest restructuring followed the acquisition of Beehives Farm in 1835.

Homestead went through several hands until, in 1812, George Olliver of West Kingston paid £5,800 for its conveyance from Thomas Shaft.[23] The whole property then amounted to just over 111 acres. It continued as part of his West Kingston estate until sold for building and brickworks in 1895 and 1897. A few modifications took place in that time certainly, with small additions from the Gratwicke estate and from Baytree Cottage. The last tenant farmer at the Homestead was John Haines, for about 37 years until his decease in 1886.

The site of the cottages was just south of the present flats. One of these would appear to have been on a 9,000-year lease, a virtual freehold,

54   East Kingston, east front, 1980.
The low south wing is the oldest part, dating from when it was the manor house of Kingston. Next to that a large 18th-century wing is built in Flemish bond brickwork with grey headers and sash windows, facing east over the garden.

dating from 1615 when it was owned by Reed. They were acquired by John Baker, as part of his Baytree Cottage estate, between 1724 and 1743, and then sold to George Henty in 1808 and so back to the Homestead in 1835.

Kingston Manor House – East Kingston and West Kingston

All other tenancies of the manor became effectively attached to the Manor Farm in the course of time, and absolutely so when Messrs Olliver purchased the manor outright in 1786. The farm was, and some of it still is, attached to the house that is now called East Kingston, which has an early wing on the south, and 18th- and 19th-century ranges north of that.

In the 1524 taxation or subsidy John Smith was the wealthiest inhabitant and probably the occupier of the Manor Farm when Kingston was owned by Tewkesbury Abbey.[24] Thomas Chambers was a later tenant who died in 1582, the Abbey lands having been sold to Robert Palmer in 1540. It was presumably soon after when Henry Roberts 'and others' took over tenancy, being favoured as a Palmer relative with a rent of £14 2s. Henry was there in 1602 until at least 1610, but by then was only in occupation of the house, the farm now let out at a greatly increased rent of £100. A number of other succeeding farmers can be deduced.

The manor windmill stood just west of the site of a future house that is now called Kingston Manor. It had its miller tenant in 1602, paying £4 rent, but was demolished before 1671 when only the mill ball or mound remained.

What is not stated is the area of the farm, but there is every reason to suppose it was in the same general location as in 1671. Less certain is that the manor house was at present-day East Kingston. It is at least conceivable it was moved there prior to 1671, due to incursions by the sea which was in process of destroying most of the village and its church.

In 1671 John Pannett was nearing the end of a 21-year lease, still at the £100 rent, when his farm was estimated at almost 175 acres:

> The Manor House called the farm house is built with stone and is situate lying and being in the Chapellry of Kingston part of the parish of Ferring in the said county of Sussex with two barns, a granary, stables, stalls, and other buildings thereunto belonging, one garden, two

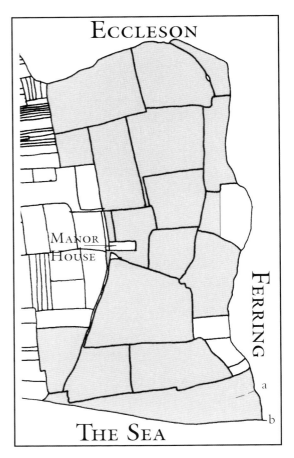

55   *Kingston Manor Farm, 1671.*

The demesne farm and manor house today named East Kingston, extending from the lakes of Ecclesden in Angmering to the sea, with Ferring Rife in its old course bounding the manor on the east. Most of the southern field has been lost to the sea. a - line of beach today. b - line of beach on 1759 map.

56   East Kingston west front, 1980.
A view of the west wing, in excellent gauged and coursed flint pebbles, and a mansard roof, presumably built in the 19th century by Messrs Henty.

closes or yards and a Hemp Platt lying all together about the middle of the Demesne Land.

From his probate inventory (see below), the house would appear to have consisted of six upper and six lower rooms, including the usual large dining hall, and conceivably a main wing and cross wing, as double piles or parallel ranges were not then usual in vernacular houses. His farm was the usual mixed arable and livestock business, with stock and implements similar to those at East Preston Farm. After his decease in 1678 the farm went to his son, until Thomas Olliver of Angmering took over for an initial 10 years from 1686, and this notable family then continued in occupation.

At some unknown date before *c.*1724 another great leasehold farm, previously Wright's, came into Olliver hands and was integrated with the old demesne lands. A few years later most of the manor was in their hands, including the old freeholds and copyholds of inheritance, the last land taken over being the old Elphick lands recently attached to Baytree House in East Preston.

In 1786, with the purchase of the manor by cousins George and William Olliver, the whole of Kingston was redistributed between them. The eastern part centred on the old Manor House, and the western at New or West Kingston, at what is today called Kingston Manor House. George's East Kingston was now massively in debt and in 1811 it was sold to Samuel Henty senior and junior, the latter having married a daughter of George Olliver.[25]

Kingstone 1678

February the 14th day 1678 A trewe and pfect Inventery taken of the good & chattells of John Pannett late of Kingstone in the cou. of Sussex yeo. deceased and praysed by Richard Jupp and George Hooke yeomen.

	£	s	d
Imprimus his wearinge aparrell and money			
in his purs	4	0	0
In the **Parler Chamber** the goods theire	47	0	0
In the **Chitchin Chamber** the goods theire	20	0	0
In the **Hall Chamber** the goods theire	9	0	0
In the **Littell Chamber** the goods theire	1	0	0
It for hemp	4	10	0
It one clok	1	0	0
In the **Servants Chamber** the goods theire	1	10	0
In the **Bruhous Chamber** the goods theire	2	0	0
In the **Parlar** the goods theire	4	0	0
In the **Hall** the goods theire	6	10	0
In the **Milkhous** the goods theire	1	0	0
In the **Chitchin**			
It for pewter & bras	5	0	0
and for other goods theire	4	10	0
It for bacon	6	0	0
It for houshold linnen	6	0	0
In the **Bakehous** the goods theire	1	0	0
In the **Brewhous** the goods theire	8	0	0
It for things not seene & forgoten within dores	1	0	0
Imprimus three oxen & 4 steares	36	0	0
It seventeene cows and a bull	76	0	0
It eleven two yearling light	24	15	0
It fourteene one yearling bease	21	0	0
It six horse and harnes	33	0	0
It sheepe and lambs	36	10	0
It foreteene hogs	10	8	0
It two fat hogs	5	0	0
It for hay	29	10	0
It for 2 wagons fore dungcarts and theire wheals	20	0	0
It for whete in the barne	52	0	0
It for barly in the barne	34	0	0
It for tares	54	0	0
It for winoing tackling	2	10	0
It for whete sowen and the plowinge thereof	25	0	0
In the **Carthous**			
one cart 3 payre of dungcart thils 8d of			
thutching rods	1	5	0
It fore planks two axes	0	8	0
It fore laders	1	0	0
It for raks	1	0	0
It eight ox yoks and fore chains	1	0	0

It fore plows and theire wheles and irons	4	0	0
It for harrows	2	0	0
In the **Furshous**			
It for hesbandry tackling and other lumber	3	0	0
It three duzen of wattells and half a duzen of heve gats	2	0	0
It for wood and fagats	7	0	0
It one grinston	0	10	0
It for things not seene and forgotten	1	0	0
Sum totall is	616	16	0

George Hooke Richard Juppe

Kingston Village

With the old village planted nearer the sea than East Preston, it was already in danger at the beginning of the 17th century.[26] It is probable that the seven 'Cotages buylte' in 1602 were provided to replace some already inundated. What is known is that in 1635 it was a 'street village' in what is now Peak Lane, with a church at the south end where a lane branched across to the manor house. This is where all the villagers appear to have had their houses, with their lands in surrounding open fields or commons. Even in 1671 one of these fields was called 'Undertown', which suggests it was a remnant of the field that extended south of the original settlement.

As all but a few house sites were lost, a detailed account of the villagers' lands is inappropriate. But the first great addition to the Manor Farm took place in the early 18th century with the lease of Wright's 112 nominal acres. This originally comprised some half dozen copyholds that cannot all be identified, largely taken over by John Wright in 1670, with the last 20 acres obtained soon afterwards from Oulder of Angmering. After John's decease in 1689 his land was taken up by three Lucas sisters of Surrey, and presumably went to Thomas Olliver thereafter.[27]

Another substantial collection of holdings belonging to William Olliver in the Colebrooke estate map of *c*.1724, were largely freeholds and copyholds that had belonged to William Oulder of Angmering, who founded the school there by his will of 1679. The eight-acre freehold had been two holdings in 1602, owned by Thomas Hills of Billingshurst and William Wolvyn of Ferring; another small freehold of three acres had belonged to William Spring. However, the copyholds of 32 acres were the main inheritance, originally occupied by Agnes Stanmer, surrendered to Oulder in 1653, and bequeathed to Olliver on condition of his paying 20s. each year to the poor of Angmering.[28] One other two-acre copyhold had long belonged to an unidentified Henry Olliver in 1602.

Kingston had only one large freehold of 57 acres in 1602, owned by Thomas Truelove of Corner House, East Preston, but previously by Henry Mychelbourne of Arundel and sometime by Frances Dawtrey of Petworth. After Truelove, the farm came to John Elphick gent, and then Walter

Elphick of Petworth, a family of particular interest locally who owned Pigeon House in Angmering. The family were still the owners in the early 18th century, but then Colebrooke, lord of the manor, must have purchased the freehold, for it became a leasehold farm occupied by Thomas May and then Daniel Simmonds. In 1773 George Olliver purchased it together with Baytree House in East Preston.[29] A 10-acre copyhold of inheritance owned by Edward Drewett in 1602 was also taken over by Elphick in 1675, and was the last part of the farm held by the family in the late 18th century.

A 12-acre copyhold, that became leasehold in 1656 for a rent of £5, was taken by Paul Laurence who also had land in East Preston. It passed to Thomas May of Baytree House, and no doubt formed part of the farm purchased by George Olliver in 1773 and already occupied by him.

It is difficult to identify two copyholds, of 12 and eight acres in 1602, that evidently passed to John Bennett junior – as distinct from senior of Ferring – some few years later, at 22s. 9d. rent. John died in 1643, followed by several generations more with the same first name. His house in 1635 was on the east side of the Street or Peak Lane, near a well that still exists. It can only be assumed that soon after 1724 this property was swallowed up by the Olliver estate.

One property that may be identifiable belonged to Richard Knight in 1602, and in 1619 brought the Baker family to Kingston a decade before they moved to Baytree Cottage in East Preston.[30] They were in time to see the chapel sink into the sea, Robert being one of the churchwardens reporting this doleful event. In the general fashion, this 15-acre property was made leasehold for 21 years in 1663 with Thomas Baker now paying £8 rent. The estate map of c.1724 is almost certainly wrong in showing this as a copyhold. Messrs Olliver were able to acquire it shortly afterwards.

That only leaves one more smallholding, some 13 acres probably occupied by Robert Wylkyn in 1602. This became the Anne Heberden leasehold prior to 1671, at £6 rent, and in 1680 passed to her son John for a 21-year term. Soon afterwards Richard Webb came into occupation, as shown on the estate map, and it went on to complete the Olliver estate in Kingston.

In the 1744 rental Thomas and George Olliver were joint tenants of Kingston Farm at £222 rent. The only other substantial tenant was Thomas May of East Preston, with the old Elphick property and its attachments, and he had only five more years of life, as witnessed by his headstone in the churchyard. Forty years later Messrs Olliver purchased the manor outright, and soon afterwards split the land between them.

57   *Kingston village well, 1981.*
Base of a well, no doubt associated with Kingston village, excavated about 500 feet south and a little east of the headland at Peak Lane, the former Street. Two courses of chalk blocks set on a timber frame remained, and several items including wooden withy-bound buckets were recovered from the silt.

10

OLLIVER AND WARREN: FROM YEOMAN TO SQUIRE

In the early 17th century Kingston was a thriving village with many copyhold and freehold farms, albeit mostly small. But Kingston Chapel and most of the village was lost to the waves before the end of the century, and the old tenures were not renewed but amalgamated into greater holdings under the remaining farmsteads.

It was in 1686 that the Olliver family of Angmering made its first foray into Kingston; Thomas Olliver took a 10-year lease of the manor farm at East Kingston, only to die the following year. Thereafter, his youngest son Thomas took on Avenals Farm in Angmering, while his eldest son William had Kingston Manor Farm, at least for a while. It was Thomas who eventually died in possession, in 1726, while holding another large collection of old farms amounting to 112 acres. These covered much of the western part of the manor, with William owning or occupying much of the remainder. William (d.1745), a son of Thomas, occupied all the family lands in Kingston thereafter, about 390 acres in the parish, besides 50 acres of pasture in Lyminster, but in 1745 his brothers Thomas and George (d.1786) took over. The main leaseholds and smaller freehold with copyhold lands were split between their two

58   West Kingston, 1872. A sales brochure drawing of Kingston House, before it was renamed Kingston Manor. This south aspect with its fine park is much the same today.

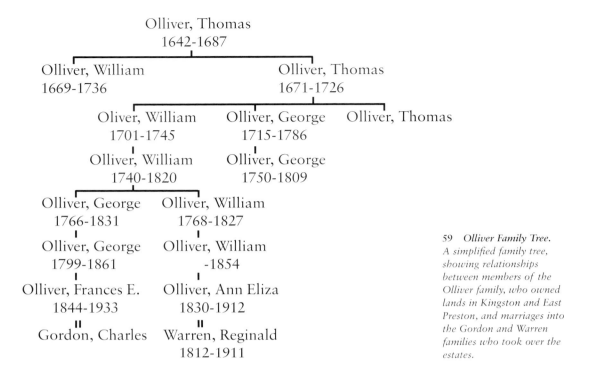

Olliver, Thomas
1642-1687

Olliver, William
1669-1736

Olliver, Thomas
1671-1726

Oliver, William
1701-1745

Olliver, George
1715-1786

Olliver, Thomas

Olliver, William
1740-1820

Olliver, George
1750-1809

Olliver, George
1766-1831

Olliver, William
1768-1827

Olliver, George
1799-1861

Olliver, William
-1854

Olliver, Frances E.
1844-1933

Olliver, Ann Eliza
1830-1912

Gordon, Charles

Warren, Reginald
1812-1911

59   Olliver Family Tree.
A simplified family tree,
showing relationships
between members of the
Olliver family, who owned
lands in Kingston and East
Preston, and marriages into
the Gordon and Warren
families who took over the
estates.

families during the rest of the century. In 1773 the last independent lease fell to George, at the manor house, when he acquired Kingston land attached to Baytrees in East Preston.

It was the next generation of cousins who took the opportunity to purchase the whole manor from John Shelley of Michelgrove, in 1786, a new house with lands in the western half being taken by William (d.1820) and the eastern half, centred on the old manor house, taken by George Olliver (d.1809). It is a slight confusion of history that the house at West Kingston is today called Kingston Manor although it is not the original manor house. After the decease of George in 1809 his share of the mortgaged East Kingston estate was taken over by brother-in-law Samuel Henty. When Samuel died in 1816, and his son in 1853, the farm passed through the hands of W. Lyon of Goring Hall, W. Freemantle, and his daughter Agnes Pretyman, until 1914.

West Kingston or new Kingston Manor estate, which soon afterwards included Homestead Farm in East Preston, descended through William's son George to his son, also George, who died in 1861. Another son of William (d.1820), also called William, occupied Corner House Farm in East Preston, and eventually acquired ownership. Of his two sons, John Duke took over the farm and demolished the old house, building Preston Place in 1838 in its stead, only to die soon afterwards. The other son, William (d.1854), had Courtlands in Goring, and his daughter Ann married Reginald Augustus Warren, who then took over and occupied Preston Place.[1]

From the 1850s onwards R.A. Warren gradually enlarged his estate in East Preston, becoming the main landowner before his decease in 1911. He had 300 acres of land, with 24 houses and cottages, out of some 450 acres in the parish. In Angmering over 170 acres, and in West Preston some 35 acres with several more cottages, completed his estate. Mr Warren's principal sons were Reginald Olliver of London, solicitor, Admiral Herbert Augustus of the Manor House, Edward Malthus, curate of Bermondsey, and Bernard William of South Africa.

Memorials at the church include the lychgate to R.A. Warren erected in 1912, a plaque in the nave to a son killed in the Boer War, and plaques to William Olliver and son John Duke of Preston Place.[2]

60   *Workhouse east front, 1856.*
A watercolour of the east front of the first workhouse serving
parishes from Littlehampton to Broadwater, abutting the Street
almost opposite the present-day county library. The Master had
his quarters to the right, and extreme left was the kitchen and
brewhouse. To the front were gardens which were surrounded
by other buildings including a school room.

11

Gilbert Union to RDC[1]

Before 1791 all local parishes looked after their own poor, by charity or relief out of the parish rates, as required by the Elizabethan Poor Laws. This had not been a problem in a village with a small population and well-to-do farms, but population in the country generally was rapidly increasing and, allied to this, old ways were changing, the corporate philosophy of commonfield and manor giving way to the commercialism of farm owners. Increasing numbers of poor were a problem for these principal ratepayers. Probably in response to the Act of 1722, several local parishes had cottages for their poor, such as Rustington Cottages next to East Preston church, but no poor law unions had been formed.

All records were soon lost of the reason for his doing so, but in 1791 James Penfold, vicar of Ferring and East Preston, was in the vanguard of those who decided to avail themselves of the 1782 Gilbert Act. This permitted parishes to form a union so as to administer poor relief by a board of guardians, each one elected by a parish which was his responsibility, with a central house of industry or workhouse where the impoverished old, infirm and abandoned children would be sent. Those able to work would be found parish work such as road mending. James Penfold was the first visitor in charge of running the workhouse.

The founding parishes consisted only of Ferring, East Preston, Goring, Burpham and the more urban Littlehampton, but within 15 years 19 parishes in total had joined, including Broadwater, of which Worthing was then still a part. Kingston did not join, being virtually a single estate with no inhabitants other than those needed as labourers. It was a closed parish, barring settlement.

It was due, perhaps, to little more than the House on the Bend Farm's being sold, and the central location of East Preston, that two acres of land was purchased there to build the workhouse with 'land fit for gardens, orchards, and the keeping of a cow'. The site was opposite the present library in the Street, but it was not the vast building that some people recall there. The first house was a more domestic two-storey range.

Times were difficult during the Napoleonic Wars, with high prices exacerbated by occasional poor harvests. Very little record survives of the house at that time, but East Preston would seem to have interned a large proportion of its poor there, not having parish cottages. In later years the parish kept to its normal allowance of two to three inmates, from a total of seventy reckoned for the whole union.

Relief outside the house in the post-war period, for those who could not labour, was similar to that in Kingston, where an old woman received four shillings a week on which to live. Nor was Kingston unique in sending its pauper children into apprenticeships, or assisting emigration to the colonies. But a peculiar labour task for the able-bodied in coastal parishes was the extraction of sand and shingle from the beach for use on roads and building work, and also perhaps for china and glass manufacture.[2]

Workhouse children received basic schooling in reading rather than writing after 1832. Otherwise the older boys were employed in making sacks, there being few adults in the house. When the 1873 workhouse was built it included a good schoolroom, but after poor reports on its standards, some ten years later, the children were sent to the village school instead.

In 1843 a Poor Law Commission investigating East Preston Gilbert Union closely scrutinised a court case concerning three teenage boys who were accused of stealing a box from an older man and then absconding. They were seen at Ferring Brook (Ferring Rife) where they had hidden it. On returning to the workhouse they were confined for three days in a passage on bread and water, the lock-up being dilapidated, and then the visitor had two of them flogged with a cane by the governor, as many as thirteen stripes each. According to Olliver this was for running away and not theft, as the court later imagined. They were taken before a magistrate, and then to trial at Petworth, where one boy was convicted and sent to prison for four days. The court was incensed at the floggings and reprimanded the governor.

James Float ran the sack manufactory, and later married the Matron when she was widowed. Ostensibly he was then the Master and in charge, although illiterate, but everyone knew the Matron was really in control. Nevertheless, the 1843 Inquiry picked up on this: 'I give the general history of the person, and show that he is an ignorant man … he was introduced rather by marriage than by any qualifications that he possesses for the office.'

It is difficult to decide how well the inmates were normally fed and looked after. Sick people then could expect little but to be waited on while they recovered or died, as in one horrendous case of a woman kept in an attic room. The investigation into this was detailed. Mr Parker had reported,

> I saw a woman, whose life was drawing to a close under most painful
> circumstances, in a dark room to which light and air were admitted only
> by a door-way, when the door was closed, the room was in darkness,

and as a most offensive effluvia was perceptible when the door was open, the state of the atmosphere with the door closed must have been particularly offensive. The poor creature had led a very dissolute life, and had often been an inmate of the workhouse. She had been in this dark room for four or five weeks, and although it was expected that she would linger for two or three weeks, her removal to another room could not be effected in the then crowded state of the house. When I spoke to her I found her almost insensible, and she could return me no answer, she groaned once or twice, and then turned round in her bed. The workhouse Master produced me a book, by which it appeared there had been frequent complaints of the want of ventilation by the medical officer.

The diet, as occasionally published, consisted largely of bread, suet pudding, meat of sorts, cheese, and weak beer made on the premises. Rather hidden was the amount of green vegetable, but since an acre of garden was attached to the house it all depends on how well this was used. Fruit was never mentioned. There is, however, no reason to imagine anyone ever starved. One inmate, asked how the food was, said 'more than I should have had with my family out of the house', but that observation would have related to minimal outdoor relief.

A great feature of the East Preston Union is that it was not subject to the 1834 Act, and remained a Gilbert Union until 1869.[3] The house may thus have been protected from the worst excesses of the better known workhouses created after 1834. Local gentry and guardians put up a fight to stave off take-over by the commissioners after 1834, claiming that this was for the benefit of their own poor, whom they knew best how

61   Workhouse north front, c.1905.
Designed by regulation, the large barracks building of 1873 faced the meadows where the library is at present. Women were in wards to the left, men to the right, families being divided. Only the high boundary wall remains of this very well-built edifice. In later years it was named North View.

62   *Workhouse outing, 1928.*
Charabancs at the entrance to North View in 1928, the Porter's Lodge in the background. The master or superintendent, William Watson, is standing at the front, with behind him Mr Broome his assistant who would take over in 1929. 'The annual treat for aged inmates .... to the Old Palace at Tarring and ... on their return a concert.'

to treat. The truth is that any kind of centralised control by bureaucrats and government was anathema. As it transpired the Gilbert foundation suffered a slow death by regulation, the taking in of unemployed men, and the enforced separation of sexes and of children, without regard for marriage or family.

Eventually new legislation required a complete system of unions under a Poor Law board, and Kingston was forced to join. A massive three-storey regulation-designed brick building replaced the old house, with men on one side, women on the other, its foundation stone dated 1873. It was designed by G.B. Nichols and built by Robert Bushby of Littlehampton. Twenty-three parishes were united, from Lancing to Climping and Houghton, and the homely parish cottages were sold, as at Rustington. As late as 1906 a second infirmary block and a nurses' home, later used by the master or superintendent as his house, were built.[4]

The workhouse survived another inquiry into conditions there, and in the 20th century life may have improved. But although the workhouse system was abolished in 1929, when the County Council took it over as a home, it was another forty years before the 'Spike' – as workhouses were commonly called – was demolished.

The origin of state hospitals was an 1866 Act which required infirmaries to be set up in workhouses such as East Preston, following an outbreak of cholera. These became open to all-comers in 1883, but the village was too small and inaccessible to justify such modern hospitals as developed at Worthing, Shoreham and even Littlehampton.[5]

In more recent times, small institutional homes for the elderly have proliferated, in what became a retirement village. Rather different was the Cheshire home at Holmbury or St Bridgets, built in 1954. This moved to Rustington in 1987, and Chermont Court stands on the site.[6]

The introduction of a rural sanitary authority in 1872 gave rise to the split between urban and rural areas, when district councils were created in 1894. The RDC covered the country parts of the union, while Worthing, Arundel and Littlehampton were boroughs and urban districts. The new council held its meetings at the workhouse, and, naturally, its name was East Preston RDC. The board of guardians, meeting at the boardroom in January 1895, now sat in the form of a district committee excluding the town members. Its area ran from Climping to Goring and Burpham.[7] In 1894 parish councils were introduced in rural parts only, taking over civil functions from the vestries.

The RDC immediately took control of minor roads in the parishes, including all of those in East Preston and Kingston. A parish account book survives for East Preston covering the closing years from 1887, with Mr R.A. Warren as Surveyor of Highways.[8] By 1898 building by-laws had been adopted under the 1875 Public Health Act, and house plans were henceforth to be submitted for approval for basic sanitary matters.[9]

63 New and Old Infirmaries, c.1910.
These were more or less in the location of flats on the north side of Fairlands Road. In the distance is the old infirmary, nearby the 1906 infirmary, next to the Nurses House in Sea Road. Wayward women occupied the far dormitories, in the days when marriage was a requirement.

Genuine local planning was not introduced for another thirty years. East Preston RDC became Worthing RDC from 1933 to 1974, when it was reorganised as Arun District.

Following local government legislation, in 1894 a civil Parish Council was created for East Preston, but Kingston being smaller only required a parish meeting until 1998, when a council became compulsory. As may be expected, East Preston had the squire R.A. Warren as its chairman until his decease in 1911.

Masters and Matrons of the Workhouse from 1812[10]

    1812 – William and Mary Sandal
    1814 – Mary Sandal
    1821 – James Float and Mary [Sandal] Float
*c.*1848 – John Imrie
*c.*1852 – John and Ann Harding
    1875 – George S. and Margaret Harding
    1899 – James K. and Elizabeth J. Sturtevant
    1910 – William J. and Laura Watson
    1929 – Percy C. Broome Miss H. Marley

64 *Workhouse staff, after 1910.*
Staff at main north entrance, when the workhouse was becoming more like a hospice. Mr Watson, the master, and wife, the matron, are centre front. It is probably Dr Alexander at the rear. The porter Mr Gent and wife are right, their daughter Miriam giving her name to a charity raising funds for Littlehampton Hospital.

12

Coast Blockade to Coastguards[1]

The Admiralty Coast Blockade to combat smuggling was inspired by Captain J. McCulloch in 1816, providing an efficient shore patrol in addition to the Riding Officers, who were often in league with smugglers. Martello towers and hulks were amongst the stations used by them on the south coast. It may be assumed that the mariners suddenly appearing in East Preston parish registers in about 1820 were the Blockade men. They needed temporary quarters and perhaps used the recently abandoned signal station at Kingston until their cottages were built in East Preston.

A lease of land by George Olliver of Kingston to HM Customs, 'whereon to erect certain buildings for … the preventive service at East Preston', is dated 11 October 1822, followed by another for extra land on 1 March 1825.[2] What became the Coastguard Cottages were for ten years known as the Blockade House, and described as the Kingston Station although in East Preston, probably because the land was on Olliver's estate.

In 1831 the service became the Coast Guard, comprising 11 mariners and their families, with Lt Richard Woolver in command.[3] Riding Officers were pensioned off. The 'Kingston and Goring detached' contingent consisted of a chief officer, four commissioned boatmen, two chief boatmen and seven ordinary boatmen. In 1841 the Coastguard Cottages, as clearly shown on the tithe map, were referred to as the Preventive House.

Conditions were tough and patrols lasted up to sixteen hours, from dusk to dawn. All promotion could be stopped for a year at a station where a run was made by smugglers, but bribery was not uncommon. When clashes did take place injuries and worse might occur. In 1832 a party of batmen from Hastings prepared for a run at Kingston (Littlehampton) during which they came into conflict with the Coast Guard, and both Chief Boatman King and John Richardson were injured.[4] Batmen were armed with cudgels to protect the smugglers coming ashore.

There is a romantic myth of smugglers running tunnels underground from place to place, but the men were much safer in open countryside

under darkness of night. Caches of goods to bribe local people may have existed, but the tales of massive altar tombs being used is also unlikely.

Due to the danger from large parties of batmen, coastguard cottages were often designed to intercommunicate for mutual defence. The Preston 'house' therefore had entrance doors into lobbies from which pairs of dwellings opened. With two rooms up and down the cottages were of average accommodation, but the young men had large families of as many as seven children. Boatmen received 3s. a day and had shares in the rewards paid for seizures, making them better paid than day labourers in the village.

65   *Coastguard Cottages, c.1910.*
The lane to the front is today South Strand. Each entrance door gave access to a lobby with internal doors to the cottages on each side. Boatman's Cottage is hidden behind the terrace.

66   *Shipwreck, 1887,* *believed to be the* SS Henrietta *beached at Kingston and later floated by tugs. Notice the sparse beach and high eroding headland. The master of the ship married a local girl.*

In the early years, to minimise fraternisation with locals, the officers in charge, and their men, were moved on at short intervals. Apart from Lt Woolver, who served to 1835, no officer stayed more than one year. Amongst their previous stations are places from as near as Littlehampton, Elmer and Shoreham, to as far as Eastbourne and Selsey. The men themselves were mariners from anywhere in the British Isles, but with a distinct flavour of the West Country and Ireland.

Sea Cottage was a tiny house stranded on the shore at the end of what is today Sea Road, owned by Gratwicke of Ham and later by Mr R.A. Warren. Jane Knight was a widow who must have moved into the cottage soon after her husband died in 1852. But, eventually, nature had its way and a story has it that,

> One stormy Sunday morning news was brought to East Preston Church, while the service was in progress, that the sea was rising rapidly and that Knight's cottage was being washed away. The clergyman immediately stopped the service and the whole congregation went rushing down to the beach. The cottage was quite destroyed.[5]

Although the dwelling may have been inundated and wrecked, it remained in good enough condition to be converted to a lifeboat house for the coastguardsmen some time after 1871. It continued as such for another fifty years or thereabouts.

By 1856 the coastguard service was transferred from the Customs to the Admiralty, and continued to be used as a naval reserve with life-saving as its usual role. The days of smuggling were not over but wholesale warfare with gangs of men had ceased. The East Preston lifeboat crew were reported in newspapers for rescuing bathers and aiding boats in difficulties.[6]

67   *Coastguards on Parade, c.1905.*
The exact date is uncertain and the officer in charge may be William Amsden or, more probably, the earlier George Biles.

A view of the east side with a coastguard, the boat, and flagstaff off picture to the right. Shrimping nets stand against the wall. The boy is the son of the photographer from Littlehampton.

Best known of the coastguard officers is George Biles. Taking up his post by 1891, he helped with the staging of concerts at the school by the church choir and others, and for many years was the umpire at cricket matches in the village. He retired to Louisa Villas until, in 1904, Mr R.A. Warren built Elm Cottage in Sea Lane for him, which was close to the Warren Recreation Ground where he served as superintendent from 1898. He has been recalled as a strict Sabbatarian, driving people out of the ground on Sundays.[7]

The 1822 deeds record how the Coastguard Cottages land was to be leased to HM Customs for 60 years at a £10 annual rent. In 1882 the lease was renewed for 21 years. By 1912 the cottages were let to civilian servants of the Admiralty, and no doubt during the First World War the men took up their responsibility as a naval reserve. Afterwards the number of stations was considerably reduced, and in 1925 Willowhayne Hotel Company had acquired use of the Boat House which was now owned by Messrs Warren. In 1924 William Hollis of Pergolas bought most of the cottages only for them to be put up for sale with his estate a few years later. It was proposed that the cottages might be made into shops, but fortunately this did not happen. Land to the east was sold to George Finch of Palm Court House and riding school.[8]

13

THE LABOURERS' REVOLT AND BUSHBY[1]

The 1830s was a decade of revolution, from Paris to Tolpuddle. Where democracy was lacking, other means of expression had to be found. In England, with the Napoleonic Wars over, lower corn prices were met by even lower poor relief. Not only in mills were machines threatening employment, but also on farms where threshing had its horse-powered engines, albeit inefficient, and a poor harvest together with unemployment could strike a spark like any tinder box. In November 1830 incidents in Kent flared up into a general southern revolt, reaching western Sussex a week later. Threatening letters hid their writers behind the fictitious 'Captain Swing' signature. Higher wages, of 14s. a week, with reduced taxes and tithes for farmers so as to enable them to pay the wages' was the cry. And many farmers were sympathetic – they had long wanted to escape paying a tithe of a tenth of their produce, in kind or cash, to the church.[2]

Large threatening mobs moved towards Arundel by 15 November but a large force of special constables put paid to them, and in Worthing some two hundred men were finally dispersed by the Coast Blockade. But the day of the small man had arrived, and next day a massive fire at Old Place in Angmering destroyed two barns of wheat; the perpetrators were never discovered.[3]

Just after this the Home Office published a notice awarding £500 for the arrest and conviction of incendiaries, quite the common thing in the days before modern police forces had been created.[4] It was then that, in East Preston, a small tiff on the 24th and, later, a beershop binge brought catastrophe. This account of the Bushby incident in East Preston is derived from extensive reports of his trial, and also from Home Office letters.[5]

On the Homestead Farm, belonging to George Olliver junior of Kingston, the harvest-home saw ricks of corn standing in the midst of the fields waiting to be threshed, valuable corn on which the country depended for its bread. One such rick stood at the corner of the Blockade Field exactly at the east end of present-day Old Manor Road. A footpath from Kingston Street ran close by, south of the Homestead, and thence through Two Acres meadow, on a route that took walkers and horsemen eventually to the church. One of Olliver's unmarried employees, Edmund Bushby, had his lodgings with Mary Burcher in a house at the west end of Two Acres, south of the present recreation ground.

Hand threshing for the farm took place in the new barns, such a one as is now the Village Hall. This arduous work with the flail might result in one man getting through three quarters (an old measure) during a six-day week and a load or ton of wheat in less than two weeks.

In view of the current ferment Olliver was cautious, recognising the need for winter employment although he had a threshing machine. On Wednesday 24th he sent for Bushby and offered him a piece rate of 4s. a quarter. Bushby replied that he should rather work at the 'Swing' rate of 14s. a week, but upon this his employer was riled and threatened to use his machine instead.

On Sunday 28th the matter had still not been settled and, after Olliver had been to afternoon service in Preston church, he was walking home to Kingston along the footpath through his farm when Bushby overtook him and an altercation took place between the two young men. The employer revoked his offer and told his man that he would get no work at all, not even parish employment. This naturally made Bushby furious, and he threatened that if he could not work by day he would do so by night, by which was understood poaching or smuggling.

That evening Edmund, with his father and brother William, went to Elizabeth Corney's beer shop in the centre of the village, directly opposite the oppressive workhouse. They remained until 10p.m. and, with the heady beer, no doubt passed comments on recent riotous events in Sussex, the fire in Angmering, and the character of country gentlemen. Whether a plot was concocted is speculation, although Edmund's request for better wages may have been made to test whether Olliver would submit to similar demands from family men in the village. Whatever the case, in the half-hour it took for the brothers to get to their homes, on what was ordinarily a 10-minute walk, Edmund had resolved on action.

The Kingston footpath had few cottages nearby and little risk of being observed by wakeful villagers. Recklessly, Edmund borrowed a tinder-box and matches from Mary Burcher's hands, and only fifteen minutes later was heard shouting the alarm of 'fire!' along the street. Then, as Blockade men and others were dousing the blaze, the brothers were heard to say, 'Let it burn', and they wished Olliver 'were in the middle of it'.

69   Ham Manor, 19th century.
Ham Place or Manor, in Angmering, when owned by W.G.K. Gratwicke. Village cricket was played in the grounds, where there is now a golf course and estate.

70 *Edmund Bushby, 1831,*
in his round frock or
smock, waiting his fate at
Horsham.

In the sober morning light Olliver soon knew who to suspect, and Bushby's embarrassment on being questioned, allied to Mrs Burcher's testimony, was enough for Edmund and two others to be arrested and taken before the local magistrate, W.G.K. Gratwicke of Ham. Bushby was immediately committed to Horsham gaol to await trial at the next Lewes Assizes. Gaol accounts record the prisoner's miserable allowance of two pounds of bread each day, during his last weeks until 1 January.[6] And so Bushby spent three weeks locked in the felons' wing at Horsham, near the endless turnings of the hard labour machine. George Olliver wrote to the Home Secretary to ask for a Bow Street Runner to investigate the case, and a man named Johns was sent, but with no known result.[7]

In the week before Christmas 39 prisoners were transferred to Lewes for trial on various charges. The trial began on 21 December, with no substantial evidence apart from Burcher's. According to tradition, Olliver paid for witnesses to appear for Bushby, but in fact no such witness is recorded; on the contrary, his brother was at the trial, and might have been called, but it was felt that brother should not be set against brother, as would have happened in cross-examination. It is also believed that Olliver paid for the defence counsel, although he could only cross-examine prosecution witnesses.

In his summing-up the judge admitted that the evidence could only be circumstantial in 'deeds of darkness'. Then the jury withdrew and in a few minutes returned a verdict of 'guilty'. The judge proceeded to address the culprit, informing him that the offence was one for which the enacted punishment of death was seldom commuted, and he must be made an 'example'.[8]

An entirely false latter-day story linked Bushby and the crime with a youth named Goodman. This youth, only 18 years of age, was indeed convicted at the same assizes, but for firing a barn at Battle.[9] On Christmas Day, both Bushby and Goodman were conveyed back to Horsham by fly, under two guards. Then on Sunday, next day, the chaplain delivered a sermon to the gathered prisoners, 'O Israel return unto the Lord thy God for thou hast fallen by thy iniquity'. By this time Edmund was reduced to a suitable state of contrition and reportedly made full confession, saying a final goodbye to his brothers and sisters at the same time.[10]

On New Year's Day he was brought out of the goal into the gaze of some hundreds of the public from the surrounding parishes. The crowd exhibited the 'greatest decorum' during the proceedings, while a company of Foot Guard paraded nearby. A scaffold had been erected, and after ascending it Bushby 'addressed the spectators exhorting them to take warning by his end', and after the chaplain had read the Lord's Prayer, the bolt was drawn. Soon afterwards his brothers carried his body home to East Preston, and three days later Edmund was given a suitable burial in the parish churchyard, as recorded in the register. There is no reason to think he was buried outside the consecrated ground, although some secluded part would have been chosen.[11] Thomas Goodman had expected to follow Edmund to the scaffold, but was told that his confession had saved him, and he would be transported instead.

Edmund was the only person to be executed in Sussex as a result of the riots, and almost every county had just one or two hangings, whatever number had been capitally convicted. Clearly the law provided penalties out of all proportion to the crimes, and only by large-scale commutation of sentences was serious trouble avoided.

A few months later George Olliver received his well-earned reward of £500 from the Treasury, the maximum payable for having successfully prosecuted an arsonist. As a person of rigorous principles, he did not wish to keep all of the money for his own use, only such part as repaid him for providing 'various witnesses … and others compensation for their time, trouble, and services in the said Prosecution'. He was now left with a residue of £250 which he decided to put partly to charitable use.

In October 1831 a deed placed the fund of £250 into the hands of trustees, in the first place to pay out suitable rewards for conviction of 'any felons who commit fire or murder in the parishes of Kingston and East Preston'; in the second place, to reimburse Olliver in the event of another fire, whether by accident or 'any wicked incendiary', and also the costs of prosecution; in the third and last place to use only the interest for 'putting out some poor boy … of Kingston or East Preston an apprentice to some useful trade … from the most industrious and deserving families'. No doubt was expressed in the deed regarding the morality of the Bushby conviction and punishment; he was 'tried and duly convicted … and hanged for the said crime'. Any idea that Olliver felt shock at the severity of the sentence could be dispelled, unless his public face hid a very different private one.[12]

The story that his brother William was forced to leave the village as a suspected conspirator is erroneous. None of the family went away, apart perhaps for Stephen, who has no mention in the incident. The father died in 1857, and William junior in 1876, long after the village school had been built with the same 'blood money'.

Generations after the event Bushby came to be seen as a virtual martyr, a natural romanticism of victimisation. A tradition, recorded in 1947, names brother William as the real culprit, but as he was a married man with children Edmund took the blame upon himself. A Rustington woman whose daughter had a birthmark on her face took the baby and touched it against Bushby's hand as he lay in his coffin, after which the mark went away; proof, if anything could be, that Edmund was innocent. Such traditions are far too good not to be true.[13]

14

THE SCHOOLS[1]

71 *School west end,* c.1905, *with part of the boys' playground. On the right is the high flint wall of the workhouse. The cart is probably that of the Rustington baker Mr Humphrey. The small room behind the pediment is the original school of 1840, its foundation stone facing the road.*

George Olliver's first charity of 1831 sat dormant for eight years until 1839; or, at least, the fund remained intact all that time, with resentment in the village dissuading possible beneficiaries of apprenticeships. Nor did a quiescent county need a village prosecution fund.

New ideas about how to treat the 'lower orders' were being developed, and Olliver himself had set aside land for cottagers' garden allotments that were to serve the village for the next 120 years. Dame schools had provided little more than child care, but the Sunday school movement and National Society were now making large strides. Earlier in the century the curate had managed a Sunday school in the parish,[2] and reading was taught at the workhouse from 1832; reading the Scriptures was desirable, but writing unnecessary. Finally, in 1839, the government became directly involved, providing grants for education.

George Olliver had his own opinion, and in 1839 founded a school charity using the abandoned £250 prosecution and apprenticeship fund. The deed does not survive, but the 1862-3 revisions leave good clues as to the original provisions. After reciting the Olliver version of the rick burning and trial, it stipulated that £250 would fund 'erection of a School Room at East Preston', and £5 interest would be 'for and in support of a Sunday School for teaching the poor Children of East Preston and Kingston to read and giving them Instruction in the Protestant Religion … with the residue of such Interest … to purchase Winter Clothing and to give and distribute the same annually on the 6th day of January in each year unto … to the poor persons … in the said Parishes …'. That residue may have amounted to £3 a year.[3]

72 *Sunday School foundation stone, 1964, in its original location on the west side. It reads:* SUNDAY SCHOOL erected 1840.

His flint-walled and slate-roofed building in Sea Road, nearly opposite where the father of Edmund Bushby lived, has recently had its 1840 foundation stone reinstated, although not in its original position. The first school was that square-roofed portion next to the road under the shade of a horse chestnut tree.

It is evident that only a Sunday school existed at first, but by 1844 a churchwarden's presentment refers to a day school as well, superintended by the vicar, but probably transitory.[4] The first teacher may have been Harriet Jupp of Beehive Cottages, who is referred to as a 'School Mistress' in the marriage register of 1841, her father having been parish clerk before his decease in 1839.

A permanent day school brought in more qualified male teachers, and an account book for the years 1847-63, saved from a bonfire at Kingston Manor, is virtually all the information that survives. The accounts ended in 1863, because George Olliver died in 1861 and the establishment had to be refounded.[5]

That there were separate accounts for the Sunday school is indicated by a regular yearly remit of cash, including the endowment of £5 'From the Treasurer of the Sunday School'. In 1850 a report by the vicar states, 'There is a Daily and Sunday School at East Preston attended by about 15 girls, and 13 boys'. These figures appear to be accurate, as the accounts seldom indicate more than thirty children attending, on average.[6]

For 16 years the whole expense of the establishment was accounted as £791 7s. 1d., a yearly average of £49 9s. 2d., most of this being the master's salary, which was as much as £1 a week until, in 1850, it reduced to 18s. with holidays at half-pay. Finally, young Henry Baker in 1858 only received 15s. a week, although raised to 17s. soon afterwards. This was average for village schools, but less than that paid to the Older's School master in Angmering.

Holidays, on half-pay, were usually four weeks in summer and two weeks at Christmas, with various holy days. The summer harvest holiday was when children went gleaning in the corn fields, providing poor families with invaluable extra bread. Over the next fifty years, whenever the harvest was late schooling was sacrificed by many families.

Masters who are named begin with J. Beckett for a period ending August 1849; the next two are not named. Then in 1855 Lock appears briefly and, from June 1855 to April 1858, C. Cooper. Henry Baker, appointed in May 1858, continued until 1876. There is no evidence for any assistants until 1849, when women were paid 2s. a week to teach girls needlework. One of these married Henry Baker and the custom for master and wife to run the school was begun. There were other occasional teachers, in particular the vicar who took religious instruction.

With no schoolhouse for the master, lodgings had to be obtained by the managers or, if he came with wife and family, a house might be rented. Unfortunately nothing is known of the lodgings used before Henry Baker.

Around 30 per cent of school income was accounted for by weekly 'pence' paid by the pupils, later certainly 3d. a week, with relief for the poorer parents; fees were abolished in 1891. The 1851 census lists only 23 village children as scholars, ranging in age from four to 12 years. Apart from the original fund, all other income came from subscriptions made by local gentry. George Olliver was supportive of the Sunday school, with 1½ guineas yearly, other family members donating various amounts to the day school. Mr R.A. Warren of Preston Place, the vicar, Mr Gratwicke of Ham and various farm occupiers were the other principal subscribers each year. The chief officer of coastguard also subscribed, one assumes in recognition of children sent from there.

73 *Sunday School, 1840. Representation of the original 1840 school room, with slate roof and knapped flint walls. It would also have had a small ventilation lantern on top of the roof.*

Henry Baker was master from 1858 to 1876, and only 18 years old when he left Older's School in Angmering. The managers found him lodgings at Seaview with Hannah Downer, and later he would marry one of her daughters. He would see the end of the private charity school when it became a Voluntary Public Elementary School under the 1870 Education Act, but it was still dependent on voluntary funding and government grants rather than rates. The Sunday school continued well into the next century managed by the vicar and his helpers.

During 1871 the School Inspector condemned the one-roomed building, only 18 feet square, in which children of all ages were crammed, and so the first extension to the school was built.[7] A generation of improvements then ensued, with the luxury of a second room in 1883, another enlargement in 1889, and a final large room on the east side in 1898 for the infants.[8]

The payment of grants was now based on yearly exam results, mainly on the '3 Rs', a system far more pernicious than present-day tests.[9] It was not until 1880 that schooling became compulsory, and then only to 10 years of age; in 1918 it was raised to fourteen. Not until sixty years ago, in 1944, did secondary education become general, with children leaving East Preston at age eleven.

Discipline also had its grades: 'One of Rev. Tripp's class was deprived of "play" as he had neglected his verse from the Bible for the second time', and 'I asked Mr Masey to keep William at home for a week as he

74   *School group, 1889.*
It can be deduced that this picture was taken in 1889, after the new room was built that year and before John Reeve arrived. This shows the entire staff and children, with Mr Counsell at the rear, Miss Hendrie left and Miss Booker on the right. Not until 1898 was the last large infant room built, when the old bellcote was removed.

had been using improper language', while, in one instance of truancy, William Beagle was brought back by his own father who requested punishment, and three strokes of the cane were administered.[10]

From this time forward elementary education in the village followed the usual course for a National and, from 1907, a church school.[11] In 1902 the county took over as the education authority funding the teachers, while the parish paid for the buildings. At this date the head teacher earned a salary of £120.[12] Plans for a new school in the 1930s came to nothing, largely because of the inability to raise funds.[13] As a result, in 1939 the county took over entirely and the school ceased to be a church establishment.[14]

Former pupils have recalled what it was like attending the school in the past:

> When I started school in 1897 or '98, it was known as the National School. My first teacher was Jenny [Jane] Booker, the daughter of the blacksmith ... she knocked some sense into us, and she was there for many years. We used to have a School Concert at the end of the Xmas term, and before the actual night the bigger boys had to process up to the Workhouse and collect Windsor chairs to help with the seating. Then we went to the Workhouse and repeated the concert for the old people.

75 *School group, c.1897.*
A remarkably glum group from the Lower Division of the school, with John Reeves the master. Only one child has been identified – Lily Hills born in 1891.

76   *School group, before*
1908.
By the beginning of the
20th century pupil numbers
had increased, as in this
picture, taken on what was
then a quiet country street.
The whole north side of
the school building is
shown, including the infant
room of 1898 to the left,
and corner of the original
1840 room extreme right.

The only means of heating was a free standing Tortoise stove, which only took the edge off the cold bitter days. Then the desks were pulled away from the wall and we all went round the room in a crocodile stamping our feet, clapping our hands, and reciting our tables.

When Queen Victoria died in 1901 we schoolboys were expected to wear a black tie and a black arm band on our left arm as a mark of respect.[15]

I went to school when I was five in 1925. Miss Booker was the infant teacher. Then there was Mrs Annie Taylor in charge of the middle school, and her husband John who was the Head Master; he had the big L-shaped room and there were three or four classes there. He taught all three sections, and there was some of us trying to learn poetry, and some trying to recite tables; it was real chaos. There was two or three boys who used to gang up and torment Mr Taylor, and then he used to get into a bad temper and I've known him lose his false teeth, and have to retrieve them from under the blackboard.

Twice a year the School Governors used to cough up the money for us to go to Chichester Cathedral, and one year the Tower of London. That was an adventure.

On every Saints Day we used to go in a crocodile across the fields to church.[16] The boys used to try and push us girls into the cow pats. Being very wicked, we enjoyed it more for the half day's holiday we had afterwards. There was a heck of a lot of Saints Days. Rev. Williams had to make sure he was doing his job and teaching us, and we were expected to go to Sunday School at church as well. About once a month he came to give religious instruction.

On Empire Day we were all marched out to the cricket field. By the Fives Court there was a flag staff, and the Union Jack was set up; all the School Governors were there, and we had to salute the flag. As we went past all the gentry and boys used to touch their caps, and the girls did a bob or curtsy. Then there was a service, and singing 'Land of Hope and Glory', and 'God Save the King'.

At the back of the school the boys shared an allotment, and there was some large apple trees. Very often the apples got pinched and they got a hiding for it. There was always trouble at conker time, with the big horse chestnut at the front of the school. Throwing sticks up at that you could break the slates on the roof.[17]

English culture, religion and history, were still a matter of pride, the atlas blazoned red where the Empire had brought safety for commerce and the navy suppressed piracy and slavery where it had previously been accepted. In the school playgrounds conkers and cricket were played in their season, and Second World War brick shelters eventually became playgrounds, their recent urgency half forgotten.

By 1951 the school had fallen far behind in standards and had become overcrowded, so that the present primary school in Lashmar Road had to be built and the George Olliver foundation ended its days, sold for commercial use.[18] The vicar's hopes that the old school might be used for parish rooms were dashed. 'After spending years in the old school

buildings, in which she managed nevertheless to maintain a spirit of happiness, Mrs Bentley has come into the new school, "The Promised Land", if only for a few months.' An infant wing to the new school opened in 1973.

Other transient private schools were founded in the 20th century, in particular at West Preston Manor under Miss Boykett from 1933-79.[19] Others included Angmering Court or Mount Roland in Sea Lane.

*77   **Sunday and Day School Teachers, 1913,** at Preston Place, no doubt in July when the children were invited as a treat, with tea and games. Top left is Walter Booker. Amy Warren is behind the curate. In the front centre is John Taylor, the Rev. Williams, and Jane Booker.*

The Head Teachers from 1858

Henry Baker	1858-76	of Seaview
Oliver Counsell	1879-89	of Preston Cottage and Louisa Villas
John Reeve	1889-1901	of Louisa Villas and Mayfield
Herbert Taylor	1901-33	of South Norris and Lashmars
May Griffin	1933-4	of Rustington
Helen Harkness	1934-44	of Louisa Villas and St Mary's
Rachel Bentley	1945-51	of Rustington
Mr Richards	1951-	took over from Mrs Bentley at the end of the first term at the new school

15

A Victorian Village
and its Houses

The character of the villages in the late 19th century may be illustrated by a description of the houses at that time, north to south along the main road and into Kingston. All of them were set in a landscape of arable farmland and pasture, with flint boundary walls or elm hedgerows along roads and lanes, and were mostly flint-faced and thatched, or slate roofed if more recently built. It was a small community, not entirely self-supporting, and relying on tradesmen delivering goods from Angmering and Littlehampton.

In the course of a hundred years, from 1801 to 1901, Kingston kept tidily to two farms and a few cottages, but East Preston underwent a small revolution. The coming of the railway in 1846, with Angmering station close at hand, expanded horizons.[1] If roads through the village in the 19th century or the 1902 tramway scheme along the shoreline had also gone ahead the effect would have been dramatic.[2] In 1801, besides the workhouse, there were only 20 households, and all were either landowners, tenant farmers or farm workers, or in allied trades such as blacksmith. By 1901 there were 76 households present at the census but

78 *Coachmans Cottage, early 20th century.*
South side of the cottage, built 1836 in similar style to the old school, with flint facings and stucco window surrounds. There are flats on this Worthing Road site today.

only one person gave himself as a farmer and he was Mr R.A. Warren, a gentleman farmer if ever there was one. The villagers included his bailiff and some 17 others in farm trades from carter and shepherd to labourer, with, as ever, the blacksmith. A new sort of grower had appeared in the market gardener, or nurseryman, with 10 households. Another less popular trade had recently arrived in the brickmaker, with eight households. Ten coastguards still occupied their row of cottages after eighty years. Three gardeners were needed by the gentry, while a medley of individuals included a school teacher, tutor, saddler, paper hanger, innkeeper, postman, coal merchant, laundress, court bailiff and dairyman, police constable, stock broker, and 14 others retired from all sorts of trades and profession.

Preston Place was the principal residence in the village during the late 19th century, built by

79 *Preston Place windmill, c.1905, built above farm buildings at the top of the Street, next to Coachman's Cottage. The entrance to Preston Place (Preston Hall) was just south of this picture.*

80 *Apple Tree Cottage, c.1905.*
A general view of the Street, looking north, with Forge Cottage on the right and Apple Tree on the left.

81   *Albert Booker, before 1927.*

The blacksmith and sexton of Forge Cottage standing at the church lychgate.

John D. Olliver to replace Corner House in 1838 after his mother Phillis died there. It descended to Reginald Augustus Warren, who married a daughter of her son, William of Courtlands, Goring, in 1850.[3] Mr Warren occupied this small mansion from 1855 until his decease in 1911, with several servants living in. During the First World War it was taken over by the military and used to house German POWs. On being returned to the Warren family it was put up for sale in 1920.[4] It was eventually converted to flats and renamed Preston Hall. The east wing is the original 1838 house in classical style, but the three- and four-storey west wing of 1865 is more typically Victorian. Wooded grounds to the south had large holm oaks and other trees, and a rookery high in the branches resounded with raucous cawing until the last vestiges of countryside disappeared.

Coachman's Cottage on the north side of Worthing Road, where the flats are today, was built in 1836 by John Duke Olliver and demolished in 1963, when the surrounding meadows had gone. The cottage had cart sheds behind, and to the east a threshing barn with cart and cattle sheds facing a yard. A small windmill of 1853 surmounted the barn, working a pump taking water to Preston Place, as well as grinding corn, but it ceased operation about 1916. As the name indicates, it was originally occupied by the Preston Place coachman.

In Worthing Road is **The Hollies**, or Groves' Cottage, built behind Preston Place in about 1854 for the farm bailiff William Groves. It was used as such until Mr R.A. Warren gave up farming in 1910, although Jacob Wheeler had the superior title of farm steward in 1891. South of the mansion in the Street is a pair of flint cottages, **Apple Tree** and **Jasmin**, which were built for the farm servants of William Olliver in 1810. They were not sold by the Warren family until after 1942.

Forge Cottage did not acquire the village blacksmith business until early in the 19th century, the Booker family being in that trade for three generations, beginning with James and continuing with his nephew Albert who died in 1927 and, finally, Albert's sons. A daughter of Albert was a teacher at the village school. The forge itself, as may be seen in many old photographs, was situated against the road north of the cottage. The house was part of the Bay Tree House Farm, which Mr R.A. Warren

82   *Wistaria Cottage,
1980, very much the same
in external appearance as it
was in the 19th century.*

purchased in 1863 and his family sold to Mr Langmead, before the site
was acquired by developers in 1957. The last blacksmith was Mr Cozzi,
although the cottage was occupied by Walter Booker, the band leader
and church organist.

Wistaria. A 19th-century name for this flint and thatch house is
Farley's Cottage, after Charles Farley, a manor house farmer whose wife
was a school teacher. After 1876 it became a cottage in the Warren estate
when he purchased the Manor Farm. In 1891 Thomas Stafford lived there
as the farm bailiff. On the decease of Mr E.M. Warren in 1942 the house
was sold to its tenant, Mr Wright, a smallholder and greengrocer. Just to
the north, where are now modern bungalows, was **Gardeners Cottage**,
built about 1860 for the Preston Place gardener.

Going south, past meadows and Parsons Way footpath from the
church to Ferring, **Barn Row** was situated amongst the Manor House
farm buildings, and may perhaps have been a conversion from one of

83   *Barn Row, c.1905.
View from Bay Tree
croft across the Street
with Manor House barn
beyond.*

84   *Admiral Warren,*
before 1926.
He lived at the Manor
House from 1913, after his
father and mother died at
Preston Place.

them in 1849, with farm labourer occupants. Originally five cottages, they were sold to Mr Langmead after E.M. Warren died and, on being demolished over twenty years later, were replaced by the present Barn Row bungalows, owned by the District Council.

The ancient **Manor House** was rebuilt as the present double pile building presumably during the 18th century, in knapped flint with a tiled roof. During much of the 19th century it was two dwellings, occupied by the Corney family, reverting to one house in 1913 until after the Second World War, when it became Midholme, Old House and Tutts Cottage. Today the main house is converted to flats, but Tutts Cottage is separate at the north end. In 1876 Edward C. Holmes sold the property, including 27 acres of land, to R.A. Warren.[5] His son, Admiral Warren, occupied it in 1913, building the south extension, and after he died in 1926 it was sold to Mrs Barnard. In 1891 it was called the Shepherd's House and occupied by William Sharp, with part of it the village Reading Room.

The only house in Sea Lane was the **House on the Bend**, with its farm that R.A. Warren purchased from John Batcock in 1865. Subsequently used as cottages, it had one of his shepherds living there, until conversion back to one dwelling before the last war. What there is left of the farm buildings became riding stables and, until recently, a veterinary business. A small thatched building by the road has a 1723 datestone with the initials of Thomas and Mary Green.

85   *House on the Bend,*
20th century.

It was not until 1887 that **Far End** arose at the south end of Sea Lane, owned by the artist Henry Holiday. The author, Israel Zangwill, lived there from 1906 until 1926, and then his widow. The stables to the south have recently been replaced by a bungalow.

Baytree House and farm buildings, with its farm, was purchased from the Gratwicke family by Mr R.A. Warren in 1863, before the main Gratwicke estate sale of 1868.[6] The tenant farmers departed and it was let to a succession of retired gentlemen. Major Andrews RE lived there before the First World War, and the Rev. Orme of Angmering with his family from 1913. The present stuccoed building is early 19th-century, with an early 20th-century east extension. The large walled kitchen garden is occupied by bungalows.

Southsea Cottage has its name above the rustic porch and was presumably built by John Harding when he became trustee for the Slater estate. He lived there after he retired as workhouse master, and was succeeded by his widow. In 1901 this became the sub post office, under Mr Charles Challen jun., when the telegraph came to the village, but in 1911 it moved to York House.[7] The stationmaster at Angmering was in charge of the sorting office for local villages until 1919. A telephone service arrived in 1912 when an exchange opened at Rustington Post Office. Other basic services took a few more years, with gas in 1909, electricity to the workhouse in 1926, street lighting by the Parish Council in 1928, and by mains drainage and water shortly before the war. It is also notable that modern street names were not settled until 1949 when Preston Street became Sea Road; Sea Lane had been previously agreed.[8]

Forge House or the **Rosery** is where the first village beer shop was from 1830 until 1850, when it passed across to the *Three Crowns*.

86 *Israel Zangwill,*
the author, when resident at
Far End.

87 *Southsea Post Office,*
c.1910.
The village post office until
1911, seen with what is
believed to be F. Challen
and others of the family.

88 *Postmen*, c.1904.
*Serving the local villages
are Bill Edmunds, George
Corney of Preston
Cottage, with beard, Jack
Graysmark, and Jack
McDonald. All but George
lived at Angmering about
that date.*

89 *Forge House*, c.1960,
*with wrought iron work at
what may once have been
a blacksmith's forge under
Charles Hills, and was
certainly the Hardy studio
early in the 20th century,
with its north light.*

Although dating from the 18th century, the original building is almost
lost amidst the modern extensions built by Heywood Hardy in 1909 and
1913, including the whole of the east wing. A small barn by the road,
used by Hardy as his studio and later as a workshop making wrought
ironwork, was demolished in 1971, when the house was a restaurant. In
2005 it was again extended and altered.

90   *Engineers Cottage, 1970, in the Street when part of the workhouse, before alteration and renaming.*

The original **Workhouse** for the impotent poor from the Union of local parishes was a small two-storey flint and brick building. When the Local Government Board took over administration in 1871, a new architect-designed house was constructed by 1873 with a vast three-storey brick central block, and various other later wings. The main building faced north towards the present library. It was taken over by the County in 1929, and finally demolished in 1969. In 1891 it had some 150 inmates from the various parishes in the Union, with George Harding and his wife as master and matron. The site was sold in 1970 for £98,000 to be occupied by Fairland Road and estate,[9] the only surviving parts being the high boundary walls and stables converted to the Engineer's Cottage in 1924 but now a private house.[10]

The two **Slater's Cottages** were adjoining, although only the one erected in *c.*1851 survives. The 1870 house was demolished and the site occupied in 1928 by a butcher's shop, which is now a restaurant. In 1891 Charles Barnard had a cottage shop there. The houses had belonged to Henry Slater of Preston Cottage.

Preston Cottage, on the corner of the Street and North Lane, was built by John Slater in 1810 on land his wife inherited from the Corney manor house estate. His son Henry died there in 1869, after which the estate passed to Mr Harding as trustee for George Corney, who occupied the house from about 1875. George was variously a school attendance officer and postman, who died in 1924. A transient brickworks on the Slater farm, by the beach east of Sea Lane, may have supplied bricks for this and other houses, including Preston Place in 1838. The walls are faced with excellently laid coursed and gauged flint pebbles.

On the other corner of the Street was the *Three Crowns* inn, the only public house in the village, and meeting place for many of the village clubs. The ancient Winters house that became a beer shop about 1850, under Sarah Knight and later her son-in-law Henry Farmaner, had been here. Constable & Son took over ownership and 'restored' the premises in 1872 as the *Three Crowns* inn, and it continued under them until 1938, when the new *Three Crowns* opened in Sea Road, only for that to close for good 60 years later in 1998. East Preston and Kingston British Legion officially separated from Angmering in 1938, under the presidency of Col Johnson, occupying the old pub in 1947, buying it in 1949 and building a large extension in 1990.[11]

91 *Workhouse foundation stone, 1873, in the central clock tower of the workhouse over the main entrance facing the Street.*

BEER SHOP at ROSERY (opened 1830)

Elizabeth Corney	1830-1843
Henry Slater	1843-1850

Approximate date of transfer to present British Legion site 1850

BEER SHOP and THREE CROWNS INN (from c.1870) at British Legion site

Sarah Knight	1850-1857
Henry Farmaner	1857-1871
House rebuilt by Constable & Sons	1872
Henry Reed	1871-1877
John Jeffery	1877-1885
Charles Maclean	1885-1890
Charles Challen (had been the Angmering schoolmaster)	1890-1908
Lucy Challen	1908-1909 [12]
Stephen H. Pocock (from Angmering)	1910-1933
Stephen J.G. Pocock	1933-1938 retired

Directly opposite Preston Cottage, where there are now shops, **North Lane Cottages** with Elm Cottage behind, was a thatched row of four cottages built by Richard Baker of Baytree Cottage in about 1810. Widow Baker had a small shop in one of them, which Charlotte Capel continued until 1900, selling a few trifles. They were demolished in about 1960 when the parade of shops was extended.[13]

York House – the **Village Stores** – constructed on what had been part of the Boxtree croft in 1886, was owned and occupied by Robert Clough, a coal merchant, until 1905, when it was acquired by grocer Frank Boswell. A shop occupied the front rooms from about 1900 and is still there today. The post office moved to 'Boswell's' by 1911 and continued there until 1926, when it transferred to The Parade. It moved to Bon Marche shops nearby in 1937,[14] and to the supermarket shop on the old North Lane Cottages site in 1999. An abortive raid took place in 1933, when the safe was abandoned as the village policeman chased off the men in their car.

92   *Village shop,* **Three Crowns,** *Preston Cottage,* c.*1905, at the junction of the Street and Sea Road. The shop sign has the name D.R. Elliott, an Angmering grocer. Next to it the* **Three Crowns** *sign can be seen. In the background is Preston Cottage with its original porch.*

93   **Three Crowns,** *1912. Stephen H. Pocock took over from Messrs Challen in 1910, and the family were in occupation until it closed in 1938. Many village clubs had meetings at a room set aside for them.*

94   North Lane Cottages, 19th century.

This drawing shows the rossel-stiles used instead of gates into the gardens, low parts of the walls that were useful in a road liable to flooding. Originally this was only one pair of cottages, as the construction suggests.

Boxtree Cottage, with its brick and flint date panel in the east end, was from 1806 owned and occupied by the Ayling family. Stephen Ayling, the parish clerk, had one half, and Ruful a bricklayer the other in 1891. In 1926 it became one dwelling again and in 1991 the old house was extended slightly west.

South of that, **Shorewell House,** later renamed **Greycot,** dates from 1871 when Henry Farmaner, the landlord of the *Three Crowns* inn, retired there after the pub was taken over by Constable & Son. Past the allotment gardens provided by George Olliver, the old **school,** presently two shops, was founded in 1840 as a Sunday school, soon afterwards including a day school. The original room is the square building nearest Sea Road.

When R.A. Warren bought Baytree Cottage in 1869, the farmyard to the north was sold to Henry Reeks, a son of the Angmering vicar, who built **Lorne Villa** in 1871. In 1917 it was taken over by the workhouse when that institution was a hospital for wounded soldiers.[15] Nurses' accommodation erected there in 1932 became the present Martlets

95   Boxtree Cottages, c.1910.

The villagers have been named as Esther, Emily, and their mother Mrs Stephen Ayling, with F. Challen and boys Reginald and Mafeking Legg. This house has been kept very much as it was, although with a recent western extension.

home for the elderly in 1957, but is soon to be rebuilt. Lorne Villa was demolished after the Second World War.[16]

Baytree Cottage is a small 16th-century timber-framed house, owned and occupied by the Baker family from about 1630 until Richard Baker died in 1842. It was acquired by R.A. Warren in 1869. There were several occupants before William Farmaner was there from about 1890 until his decease in 1918. In 1891 and later he was a county court bailiff and dairy farmer. Thomas Chatfield acquired ownership in 1920, having his carpentry shop at the rear and newsagents shop by the road. Mr Eschbaecher, a recent occupant, was responsible for the restoration of this house and Boxtree Cottages.

97 *Hurdles villas, c.1905. The Hurdles to Mayfield row of villas was built by Thomas Jarrett of Angmering over several years to 1902 and marks the beginning of modern suburban East Preston.*

98   *Beehive Cottages,*
c.1965, before restoration,
with rifle range beyond.
Notice the old street lamps
installed by the Parish
Council.

Jackmans Cottages, a flint-faced row of four, replaced a small cottage on its site in 1873, when it was owned by Mr Harding, the workhouse master, later of the Homestead. They were reputedly built of material from the old workhouse, demolished about that time. John Envers, the village policeman, had one of these in 1891. **Louisa Villas** in the croft behind Jackmans Cottages are of later date, Mr Harding's farm bailiff being an occupant in 1881, and one of them was later the home of the schoolmaster John Reeve until 1896, when the school managers acquired Mayfield, one of the new villas near the Homestead, for him. In those days it was thought sensible for the community to provide houses for its key workers and others.

Beehive Cottages, the former farmhouse, was reduced to cottages in 1835, when the farm was taken over by the Homestead. In 1893 R.A. Warren acquired some 75 acres with the cottages, which were held by his family until 1945.[18] Its barn built *c.*1800 is now the village hall and croft the cricket field. Harry Boxall, a rifle range trustee, was one of the well-known occupants.

The Homestead, almost hidden behind its farmyard and barns, was once the principal farmstead in the village after the Manor House. In the 19th century, when owned by the Olliver family of Kingston, it had more than one hundred acres of mainly arable land. The last tenant farmer was Mr Haines, who died in 1886, after which R.A. Warren of Preston Place

leased the land. In 1895 the farm was broken up, and George Harding, retired workhouse master, purchased and then sold much of the land, retaining 28 acres. The house was unfortunately demolished shortly after his daughter died in 1958. Very little is known about two small cottages near the Homestead, which ceased to be inhabited after the First World War, a foundation stone in a garden wall being all that remains.

Nelson's Cottage and the **Graperies Nursery**. George Barnett established the first local market garden and glasshouse nursery in 1850 on land acquired from Baytree Cottage, building the cottage there. His son Nelson lived there all his life to 1892, growing a vast variety of fruit and flowers, including a dozen types of apple, grapes, fruit trees and pot

99   Vine Cottages, early 20th century.
The east front of the large north cottage, which still exists, with Mrs Ayling. Three to the south have been demolished.

100   Vicarage House, c.1915, soon after being built. The first house in the lane was extended east as more were constructed south of the church.

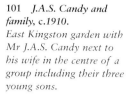

101 *J.A.S. Candy and family, c.1910.*
East Kingston garden with Mr J.A.S. Candy next to his wife in the centre of a group including their three young sons.

plants, sending them to market by rail.[18] The business was taken over by Hubert Gray who expanded it with the well-known Mr St Leger Blaauw as partner. The nursery was demolished in 1934 when Bon Marche shops and eventually Normandy estate were constructed on the site. The three small **Vine Cottages** were built soon after Nelson's, but the surviving house not until 1895.[19]

Coastguard Cottages date from 1822. In 1831 a complement of 14 men included the chief officer, and three boatmen manned the Goring outpost. That left 11 men for 'Kingston' station as it was called, despite being in East Preston, although in later years 10 men with their families was the norm according to census returns.

Seaview is the rear part of the present hotel, dating from 1825 and occupied at one time by John G. Heasman, who died in 1850 aged ninety-nine. He had been a customs officer, involved in 1804 in a violent smuggling incident at Kingston, and left us the story of Rust(ingt)on Park washed away by the sea in about 1800.[20] In 1934 Mr Frank Page set up the King of Clubs Company, with the house as the club and hotel.[21]

Just inside Angmering, near the railway crossing, **Roundstone** is of early 19th-century date, and was occupied by the parish curates for 50 years until 1913, when the Vicarage was built.[22] William Nightingale,

102   *East front of the East Kingston house, c.1910, with Mr and Mrs Candy, and perhaps the Wooddale beagles.*

curate and workhouse chaplain, occupied the house with his mother in 1891. The Rev. Williams was the last curate there.

At neighbouring Kingston, apart from the two principal houses, nothing but a few servants' cottages were permitted by the two landowners during the 19th century. Arable fields and meadows spread out unbroken from the crumbling headland by the sea towards distant Highdown.

East Kingston was the former manor house of Kingston, although largely rebuilt in the 18th and 19th centuries. J.A.S. Candy became tenant of Pretyman in 1901 and purchased the farm in 1914, four years later selling land to George Peskett for development as Kingston Gorse estate.[23] Mr Candy's last surviving son died in 1975. The south wing is perhaps the remnant of an early house, in the usual knapped flint with brick dressings. A much larger east wing is in typical 18th-century style, with sash windows either side of the garden entrance and walls of red brick with grey headers. The west wing is early 19th-century, with bay windows and walls faced with coursed and gauged flint pebbles, of similar quality to Preston Cottage. Charles Peachey was the tenant farmer in 1891.

A Kingston villager recalls that, before the First World War:

We loved hay-making time, and the neighbouring farmer used to give us and her own worker's children a wonderful tea in the hay, always finishing with strawberries and cream. She [Mrs Gordon of Kingston Manor] used to give us a Christmas Party too.

Mrs Candy used to give us a Christmas Party, a wonderful spread for tea in the lovely old kitchen. Then upstairs to the Drawing Room with the Christmas Tree. While we were playing games Mr Candy used to

103 *Candy family skating, 1907.*
Mrs Candy, with her sons Ivo and Geoffrey, skating on their pond in February.

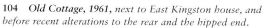

104 *Old Cottage, 1961, next to East Kingston house, and before recent alterations to the rear and the hipped end.*

have the mothers in the Dining Room to give them a glass of port or something. When it was time to go we were all given a gift off the Christmas Tree. Mr Candy also gave each family a joint of meat.[24]

The Old Cottage still exists next to East Kingston farmstead, by a reputed filled-in sawpit, and may be shown on the 1759 map, although not scheduled. It has flint walls and thatched roofed, recently much extended, but was two cottages occupied by the Braden family. Also belonging to the farm were the two early 19th-century **Lighthouse Cottages.**[25] There was no lighthouse in reality, but only a nearby signal station to warn of invasion during the Napoleonic Wars.[26] The shepherd and others lived there prior to 1916, when the houses were 'gentrified' and later sold to Millicent Payne in 1920. Binie Hale lived there later. New houses at East Kingston Farm were built by Mr Candy before he retired in 1919. Mr Sharp, his tenant farmer, then built Meadow House for himself.[27]

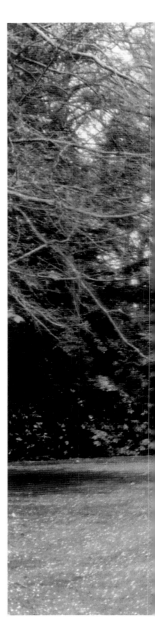

The other large house, **West Kingston**, was renamed Kingston Manor. George Olliver, who died in 1861, expanded the small house that had been on the freehold site since between 1723-43. His daughter Frances was the last of the immediate family there, having married Charles Gordon, brother of the earl. Their son John was killed on active service in 1942, leaving a widow. The house continued in decaying Victorian grandeur until after Mrs Gordon died in 1994, when it was sold and restoration began. The **Lodge** by the road is an extraordinary octagonal cottage, built to match the mansion, with stuccoed window surrounds, knapped flintwork, and parapets hiding a slate roof. It had three rooms of no particular shape and a central chimneystack. In the 1890s Charles Ansell the coachman lived there. A gardener lived in another cottage.

Some way north from the mansion the diminutive four-roomed **Rose Cottage** of the early 19th century, has recently been reconstructed. It had a thatched roof but with tiles at the eaves, and flint walls with casement windows. In the 1890s Thomas Hills the carter lived there with a large family, including Lillian who later became a pupil teacher. The large barn next to it is now a house.

Three other dwellings in Peak Lane, or Kingston Street, included **Flintstones** of the late 19th century, and a house that is now contained in **Moorings**, which may have been the Elphick farmstead in the 18th century. Otherwise all the ancient cottages, including those on the east side of the lane, have gone.

In a short twenty years or so after 1891 villagers would witness the virtual transformation of rustic Kingston and East Preston into Kingston Gorse and Angmering-on-Sea. A mere 43 farming people in the one village and 252 in the other found a sudden influx of wealth settling among and apart from them in new 'Garden Villages' that almost obliterated the old. New blood also came to the old village after Squire Warren died in 1911, when his sons took over the estate and began to sell it off.

105   *Kingston Manor,*
c.1980.
*South front of the mansion
when occupied by the
widow of John Gordon.
His mother was Frances,
the daughter of George
Olliver of Kingston, his
father Charles Gordon of
Abergeldie.*

A small community with few trades, an inn with clubroom, schoolroom used by various clubs, reading-room, a couple of cottages with parlour shops selling trifles, and a meadow where cricket could be played, after two decades of growth, had 13 new shops including a bank at The Parade with an older grocer's shop adjoining, besides a shop in the village providing most of the grocery and household goods needed by the villagers. In social terms provision was excellent, with a new Reading Room and a large YMCA, its management encouraging the creation of all manner of other clubs and facilities. South Strand also had many facilities for its own wealthy élite.

106 Parade Shops, after 1920, *shortly after being built by Mr Hollis. Unfortunately his Great War memorial plaque is not visible above the door of the bank, which closed in 2000 and is now a restaurant.*

SOUTH STRAND AND KINGSTON GORSE

For a thousand years East Preston had been a small village community, but in 1895 the process began which ended in the creation of the present subtopia. In September the sale by auction of the Homestead farm took place. Fanny Olliver of West Kingston had died in 1893 and her son Gervase, almost certainly in debt, proposed to sell both the Kingston and East Preston estates. In the event West Kingston was taken over by Colonel Gordon, who was married to Frances, the sister of Gervase. The Colonel's brother was Lord of Abergeldie.[1]

The Homestead in Sea Road, where the flats of that name are today, had 118 acres attached to it, stretching from North Lane to the sea. Mr R.A. Warren of Preston Place held the tenancy of this farm following the decease of Mr Haines, the previous tenant farmer. The Street (now Sea Road) and the extreme west end of the North Lane frontage was divided into lots for building, while the hinterland of the farm formed the principal lot, as a working farm.

George Harding acquired the farmhouse and its land and was living there by 1899 when he retired as master of the workhouse. But in 1897 he sold on a substantial portion in the north to R.A. Warren, and in the south some 40 acres to Mr Goodall the brickmaker. Thomas Jarrett of

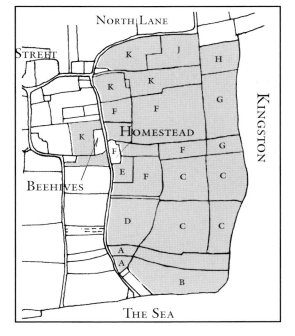

107 *Homestead, 1898, after the 1897 sale. The ancient farm had been consolidated about Homestead farmhouse, and included Beehive Farm. In 1893 R.A. Warren bought Beehive Cottages and its croft, the Cricket Field. In 1895 and 1897 the main farm was broken up. Key: a – the coastguard land owned by Col. Gordon. b – George Goodall field, shortly to become South Strand. c – George Goodall land, partly brickmaking. d – George Gotelee house, Willowhayne. e – Thomas Jarrett, the Hurdles villas. f – George Harding farm. g – George Gotelee nursery, later Frampton's Nursery. h – George Vickery house, Haven. j – Henry Havers Norris nursery and house, Shenfield. k – R.A. Warren land.*

Angmering took several of the building plots south of the Homestead, and immediately after 1895 began building villas there. Two of them were used as the first substantial guest-house and hotel in the village, named Fairview, from about 1909.[2] By 1899 development of Manor Road had begun on the Goodall brickworks land, while glasshouse nurseries and houses took over the Norris field adjoining North Lane.[3]

What proved to be the most significant development took place near the Coastguard Cottages, where after 1907 the Tamarisks, Kingmere and Salona formed the nucleus of South Strand.[4] It was in 1910 that William Hollis, already an established estate builder at Finchley, came to East Preston on holiday, staying at the Tamarisks. Goodall had sold

108 Fairview Hotel, c.1920s.
Two of the Jarrett houses converted to a hotel south of the Hurdles in Sea Road.

109 *Sports Club, after 1914.*
The original single-storey club of six bays with parapet. The houses adjoining, in Club Walk, have taken in much of the frontage as gardens in recent years.

110 *William Hollis.*
The developer of South
Strand, of the Bungalow
and later the Pergolas, and
'Mayor' of Angmering on
Sea.

up his brickmaking business in 1908, and a large part of his land came onto the market, but the making of bricks seems to have carried on for some years after. In 1911 Mr Hollis purchased a section of South Strand from Messrs Butt and built his first house, The Bungalow, as his country retreat.[5] He lived at the Pergolas after the First World War, when his estate had developed. Tennis courts and a clubhouse were constructed nearby on seaside plots extending through to Kingston.[6] In 1939 there might even have been a church on the estate but for the Second World War.

In 1913 Hollis really got going, buying a large 'green field' site north of South Strand road, which reached as far as houses south of Manor Road. He put forward plans for a Garden Village which at first envisaged 286 concrete houses, with a golf course and pier, but was fortunately transformed into the present Angmering-on-Sea estate based on self-build houses in plots set out on his estate plan.[7] Amongst the 1913 houses were Sheencot for Mrs Goode, Seacot for Mrs Dewilde, Arden for Miss Shakespeare, and Melita for Wynstanley, previously of the Tamarisks. In fact, the north side of South Strand was the extent of development before the war. Roads, landscaping, drainage, water tower and sea-wall were built first, the clubhouse and other social facilities not getting under way until 1914.[8]

William Hollis gave his own account in 1916, when he first introduced the name Angmering-on-Sea, despite opposition.[9]

> Wishing to escape from the world of bricks and mortar, I was heading for the south coast, Bognor or thereabouts, [when] I took the wrong road, though it finally proved to be the right one. My eyes had been opened by two houses in an area of thirty acres overlooking the salt-sea Channel, with a beautiful background of downs and a foreground of ocean blue. So I took a 'Tamarisk' on trial for six weeks.

111 *Southstrand Garage,*
c.1930, at the Circle, with
Mr Denyer, taxi driver
for Mr Goode of nearby
Sheencot.

I came to the determination to stay on, when a cloud made its appearance, in connection with a scheme to erect a fever hospital in the hinterland.[10] I had intended originally to put up an ordinary seaside bungalow at the cost of three or four hundred pounds, when I found myself compelled to buy the twenty-five acres opposite. We had seen bungalow towns but never an ideal garden city by the sea. First there was the making of roads forty feet wide, with grass borders and beds of shrubs. Next I put in the most approved system of modern drainage. Then came the question of water. I sank a large artesian, and built a water tower on the lines of an old Dutch mill. Gas was laid on. Next it became necessary to protect the practical from erosion of the sea. This necessitated a sea-wall 275 feet long, and additional groynes.

Then came the ornamental, the making of tennis courts, a croquet lawn and bowling green. Then the planting of trees. When war broke out I had a staff of over a hundred men working on the development. In a single night, the development came to a stop. However, the estate profited by my misconception of the World War. I expected it to be over within a few months. The result was the building of the club house, which always figured prominently in my scheme. I had the good fortune to secure the contents of a very smart little West End club 'broke in the wars'. So now Angmering-on-Sea is carrying on as happily as possible, and it looks forward to a golden future when peace shall once more bring good times back.[11]

Edwin Goode's garage was of particular interest, a large commercial establishment where he had his well-known Ford 'little bus' to serve the locality, and a taxi service. A licence for his motor char-a-banc was issued in June 1917, and by 1921 the business was known as The Downs Motor Transport Co. Ltd.[12] Goode lived at Sheencot, South Strand, backing onto The Circle where his garage was.

Over the years from 1919 to 1927 further land was purchased, reaching finally to Coke Lane, now Vermont Drive, the last purchase being the small estate that had belonged to R.N. Fairbanks of Vermont House, an American with a business in this country, whose daughter later had the new *Three Crowns*. Also included in 1926 was the Golden Acre area of Kingston previously owned by Mrs Gordon of Kingston Manor.

With so many new residents, the need for shops became urgent, and in 1920 Mr Hollis built The Parade south of the present Village Green.[13] The clock on the corner has below it his private memorial plaque to the men killed in the First World War.

The Sports Club at South Strand was one of the first amenities provided by Mr Hollis, in 1914. The original building was single-storey; its entrance portico with three Tuscan-style columns faced east, under a parapet roof:

> The club, which has its large recreation hall with stage and gallery, gentlemen's lounge, ladies' room, card room, etc., has also a fine roof garden with shelters, from which it commands magnificent views of the sea, as well as wooded country and the Downs. There are all sorts of indoor and outdoor amusements for members and friends.[14]

This clubhouse was extended in later years and transformed entirely, in 1928, into a two-storey building in Tudor style. It reopened as the Angmering Court Country Club in July of that year 'enlarged out of

113   Angmering Court Club, 1938.
View from the east of the club at its maximum size in 1938. This building was damaged and demolished in the war.

114   *Angmering Court Club, 1938.*
North side of the club at its maximum size, with Club Walk houses, most of which were attached to it.

all recognition. In addition to its other amenities it now has sleeping accommodation for about 45 members ... managed by the Southstrand Sports Club Syndicate.' An exotic air was provided by the palm trees in the grounds, illuminated by external lighting.

In 1932 and 1934 Mr Hollis put those parts of the estate he still owned up for auction at the *Old Ship Hotel* in Brighton, most of the sites having already been sold freehold to incoming residents.[15] The most interesting properties were the site of the tennis courts north of The Parade shops, the shops themselves, the Court Stables to the east of the shops, all but three of the Coastguard Cottages, Vine Cottages, the new tennis courts at Homelands Avenue and the clubhouse there, part of Palm Court terrace and the green in front, the lawns east of Pergolas scheduled as open space; the Angmering Court Club and the Lido.

115   *Sports Club Dining Hall, before it was enlarged as Angmering Court.*

Angmering-on-Sea Ltd was wound up in 1939, and Mr William Hollis died in 1948. His ashes were presumably scattered, as he wished, on a garden of remembrance at the Shakespeare bust. This had been erected in the triangle at the end of Seaview Avenue following several years of the Shakespeare Festival after 1922, funds from which were used to supplement the vicar's income.[16]

The sorry end of the clubhouse came in 1940, largely because the Army, in occupation of the coastal region, demolished groynes at this exposed point. In April it was reported, 'The

116 *Shakespeare bust, 1923,* at the south road island of
Seaview Avenue, erected in 1923 during the Shakespeare
festival which raised funds for the church over several years
from 1922. Mr Robert Atkins of the Old Vic unveiled the
memorial.

promenade which used to adjoin the Angmering
Court Marine Club was completely washed away
by the tide last week, and now it is feared that
unless further steps are taken the foundations of
the club itself will suffer.' In July, as a result of
the closure of the beach and promenade to the
public, general club facilities in the area ceased.
The whole southern half of the clubhouse was
subsequently demolished, and a small part that
remains is now a private house.

Meanwhile another affluent estate came
into being in the east of Kingston. J.A.S. Candy
owned East Kingston Farm, and in 1918 sold
the southern part of this land to the Angmering
builder, George Peskett. It does not appear that
much building took place until after 1920. The
first plans for the estate were submitted late
in 1919, but were not approved by the RDC.[17]
Scribble magazine noted in January 1917 that
George Peskett and John Phillips were planting
out the gardens of the first house at Kingston
Gorse in what was humorously called 'Kandy
Town'. It has to be assumed that development
had begun in a small way long before the main
area of the estate was purchased and roads
were laid out.

117 *Angmering Court Club promenade, 1938.*
The terrace adjoining the club house, when the resort was
at its height of popularity. Kingston is in the distance.

118   *Sea Lane House, 1980.*
South end of the wing 'on stilts'. A view of the west side would reveal the contours of this modernist building in Kingston.

One of the first houses erected was Inverfering in 1922, then Kingston Gorse House. South of it by the sea, Wharemoana, later called Kingston Hoe, was owned by John Phillips, presumably after he left Salona, East Preston in 1917. George Peskett himself then moved to Kingston, to a house at the north side of the estate called Imray. The estate water tower next to it is still very much in evidence. A spate of construction followed so that by 1931 there were some 34 dwellings in place, with most of the prime seashore sites taken. It was soon afterwards that the theatrical influx took place, bringing members of the Crazy Gang and George Black.

At the same time a number of modernist houses were built in the neighbourhood. Many of these have been altered out of all recognition, with tiled roofs and cladding replacing flat roofs and white walls. Most notable of them all is the 1939 'House on Stilts', or Sea Lane House, in Kingston, designed by F.R.S. Yorke and Marcel Bruer. White-faced, flat-roofed and T-shaped, with a long south wing open underneath, and main living rooms above, it is very different from the original three-storey cubic design, which the RDC understandably objected to.[18]

17

THE ESTATES

Town or Local Plans and control of development came only just in time to save the Downs and general countryside from complete despoliation. If developers had continued unchecked there would be nothing of value remaining for a South Downs National Park, and ribbon development along roads would have ruined the countryside elsewhere. Locally, the 1929 plan by Arthur H. Schofield, covering Arundel, Littlehampton and across towards Worthing, provided a basis for controlled development, after which every new local plan has been a retreat. A projected population of 8,000 in the area has been allowed to expand four times, with the loss of green belts around the villages and towns. These gaps were proposed in part for recreation and sports facilities, and were a reserve that is being lost.

> The reasonable alternative is a series of self-contained communities, each separated from its neighbours by a girdle of open land. The modern seaside township of Angmering-on-Sea is itself an excellent example of this compact grouping.[1]

There was a certain naivety about transport which later plans needed to address. The idea that every town could have an aerodrome, with private people flying aerial cars on short journeys, was impossible. Inter-village roads cutting through communities – such as the main road proposed through Vicarage Lane and North Lane in East Preston, and on through Kingston to Worthing – were only narrowly averted and by-passes have saved some of the villages from horrendous traffic. Perhaps the first death from a car accident in the village was Mr A. Baker, of Southsea Cottage, in 1920.

The local plan coincided with major new development proposals in East Preston and Kingston. At the time the old village was intact, with only a scattering of new buildings, and Angmering-on-Sea formed a compact affluent estate in one corner of the parish. Large areas, once farmland, were now covered with glasshouse nurseries, but not entirely so. Undoubtedly, East Preston was at its best as a village in about 1930, before excessive development had taken place but with substantial social facilities, with a reserve of space and green belt. The highways were not gridlocked with cars, and people could enjoy walking by path or road.

With Kingston Gorse already well developed, another estate in the western part of that parish came onto the drawing boards in 1930. If plans had been realised there would have been little more than a large park left surrounding Kingston Manor.[2] The farm was owned by Mrs Gordon of Kingston Manor, and only a small attachment to Angmering-on-Sea at Golden Acre was already under bricks and mortar. Peak Lane and lands to the south-west of East Kingston were all included in the proposals, and the southern part of what is now Golden Avenue would have been a crescent off the west side of a main road running south. Other roads were to run north from Coastal Road on the east side of Peak Lane. It was no doubt the intervention of war that curtailed development, and after it local planning did become concerned about infilling between the villages.

The small Kingston glebe field was also developed, but exchanged for land east of the Vicarage. However, in 1937-9 the Vicarage Lane land was sold to raise funds to invest for the vicar's income.[3] The Temple Church Choir had erected a large hut at Roundstone in 1913 for their summer camps by the sea, and in 1930 this was given to the church and moved to Vicarage Lane, only to be abandoned with the land. [4]

At that same time, with the passing of the Warren family, the greater part of their considerable estate in East Preston and Angmering came under the hammer. The most significant effect on East Preston was the creation of Willowhayne estate, between the sea and the church, from 1930 onwards.

119   *Temple Church bungalow 1913, soon after it was built, no doubt during the first summer holiday. It was sited south of the Roundstone Crossing where the garage and houses have since been built.*

120   Willowhayne Hotel,
c.1920.

*The Gotellee house, on the
corner of Manor Road,
soon after it became a
hotel, and before new
wings were built.*

In 1900 George Gotelee, who two years earlier had founded East
Preston Nursery in Vermont Drive, built himself a substantial house
in Sea Road called Willowhayne.[5] After he died in 1918 the house was
acquired by Mr Hollis and became a hotel, the nursery being taken over
by Joseph Frampton, a Worthing horticulturist.[6] The hotel expanded
vastly in size over the next 10 years.[7] Notable tennis tournaments were
held on the land to the south which, in about 1960, became the Village
Green. Finally Roper Spyers acquired ownership, until in January 1930
a disastrous fire ravaged the building. Fire brigades from Littlehampton
and Worthing were hindered by a lack of mains water, and had to run
hoses from the distant workhouse, by which time it was too late.

Roper Spyers now had capital in hand, presumably from insurance,
and an eye for new projects. The name Willowhayne, which had been
that of a house in the village, was transferred to a large housing estate
in another part of the parish – in a conveyance between R.O. Warren
and Roper Spyers, to Willowhayne Estate Ltd – in 1930.[8] A total of 118
acres of the Warren estate changed hands and soon afterwards it was
announced,

> Willowhayne Estate, with its long private sea frontage, is being developed
> along select and novel lines ... new roads are reminiscent of old
> country lanes, the object of all this being the permanent retention of
> the country-by-sea atmosphere ... entirely virgin country, parklike,
> pastoral, altogether delightful and bounded by the sea on the south,
> and the Downs on the north.

Mr Spyers also envisaged building a hotel in Pigeon House Lane, but
financial difficulties seem to have precluded this. He also acquired West
Preston Manor, but this he sold to Miss Boykett in 1933 for a private
school.

The intervention of the Second World War brought activity to a temporary halt, by which time a number of large Arts and Crafts-style houses had been built, mainly in Tamarisk Way. The central area was still farmland, though some roads were laid out. Development picked up again after the war, with more modest houses, and was only completed in the late 20th century.

The needs of ordinary villagers had not been entirely forgotten during those decades of two wars and uneasy peace. The first public housing was that provided by the District Council after the First World War, in a half-hearted attempt at making a 'nation fit for heroes'. In 1917 the Local Government Board asked councils to consider post-war housing needs for the working class. Mr Hollis, later a member of the District Council, noted in *Scribble*, 'For ourselves, we welcome any idea that will do anything to benefit the housing of the working man.'

It took until 1921 for a site to be negotiated in North Lane, two acres of land to be bought from Messrs Warren, for four houses to rent. However, the scheme was cancelled and the site was thereafter developed by the Angmering builder Mr Doddington. It was not until 1925 that another two acres was purchased near Elm Avenue and four pairs of houses built by the RDC. Then, in 1928, the Somerset Road estate was begun, on land previously owned by Mr Slater of Preston Cottage. The name of the road was undoubtedly adopted from that of the Sussex landowner and East Preston RDC chairman, A.F. Somerset.

As at Willowhayne, it was the break-up of the Warren estate that brought massive change in the north of the village. In 1932 the Rev. E.M. Warren sold the bulk of his father's estate to James Langmead of Yapton.[9] Almost immediately Mr Langmead recouped his outlay by

121 Willowhayne Hotel, *before 1930, at its greatest size, with the main hotel now built onto the south side of the original house (at the far end). Willowhayne Crescent is to the south side, where tennis courts were sited.*

122   *Former Nurses House and School, Sea Road 1969, later used by the superintendent, or master of the workhouse, after it became a County Council home. Fairlands junction occupies this site today. The old school is in the foreground.*

selling off portions of the land to developers, one series of transactions involving the entire area between North Lane, Worthing Road and the Street. The small private estates at Clarence Drive and in North Lane still left a considerable tract for recreation grounds and a new school, which became the subject of town planning. In 1937 over 33 acres, representing the bulk of what remained undeveloped, was bought by Worthing RDC from the owner. This included land eventually set aside for a recreation ground where a football ground and the new school would be.[10]

So began the Roundstone Drive estate. The pre-war houses were built at the east end of the new road, with the first of them evidently ready for occupation about the time hostilities began. The fire station, which opened in 1940 at the barn nearby, employed 12 firemen who were provided with adjacent housing.

Subsequent smaller developments have included the flats on the former Preston Place farm site, the Barn Row bungalows, and houses in Fairlands on the site of the workhouse demolished in 1969-70.

123 Far End, 1980.
The Israel Zangwill house, at the south end of Sea Lane, including the wing to the north which he built.

124 Workhouse entrance, 1965, *latterly known as North View. Two male inmates outside the main entrance gate and the Porter's Lodge shortly before its demolition.*

18

ARTS AND CRAFTS

From the end of the 19th century until after the First World War, those of independent and artistic means who wished to retire away from town but avoid popular resorts sought out unfrequented villages such as East Preston and Kingston, an open expanse of sea and beach with only a few fishermen, quiet countryside, Downs on the near horizon, and Angmering station at hand for ready travel to London.

Apart from one or two gentlemen who had retired to the village for their health, the first personality was Henry Holiday, who built Far End in 1887. A Pre-Raphaelite stained glass designer, painter and illustrator, he lived from 1839 to 1927 but did not stay long at Far End as Israel Zangwill was in residence by 1906. Zangwill became a notable figure locally, prior to his death in 1926. He wrote numerous plays and novels, some relating to the Jews. Today the only book that can be obtained from local libraries is *Children of the Ghetto*, 1899, centred on London in the early 19th century. It is reminiscent of Dickens but without the eccentricity or humour. His secretary said that,

> She did not consider him a Zionist, but he gave valuable help as President of the Jewish Territorial Organisation, which helped oppressed Jews from Russia settle in Mississippi. The Great War brought an end to its work and ten years of help by him in this movement. Among many well-known visitors to Far End were Mr Guggenheim, John Galsworthy and Jerome K Jerome.[1]

Artist Heywood Hardy came to the village in 1909 and found contentment in the Rosery (Forge Restaurant or House) which he immediately enlarged, also converting an old thatched barn into his studio. Evidently the prospect of the nearby workhouse did not deter him.[2] He was the son of a Chichester artist, born in 1842, and lived in London for much of his life. He was therefore an elderly man on coming to his last home. His forte was animal studies and hunting scenes, although he did portraiture. There are local examples of his excellent portraits in oils, and his foxhunting scenes are still popular. At the age of 83 he painted a controversial set of panels at Clymping

I AM WITH YOU ALL THE DAYS

IN MEMORIAM
HEYWOOD HARDY, WHO PAINTED FOR THIS
CHURCH THE PICTURES OF CHRISTS COMING
ON EARTH AND HIS LOVE FOR MEN·
AND WHO HIMSELF PASSED ON 1932

125   *Heywood Hardy allegorical panel, 1981.* The principal panel at Clymping church was painted in 1926.

church, depicting Jesus of Nazareth by the riverside in Sussex. A castle in the background is similar to Arundel. It is claimed that local people were used in the representations. The figures, in modern dress, include a group to the left depicting 'apathy', another 'gaiety', and two wounded soldiers portray 'suffering'. Children by the feet of Jesus represent 'purity', while a widow and her son are receiving comfort, and there is old age and a poor woman. Mr Hardy died in 1933 at Epsom and his ashes are interred at Clymping church, where the Climping panel has the year 1932.

After the First World War, Kingston Gorse estate spread along the beach greensward, business and banking being spiced up by a colourful group of theatricals in the thirties. The Gorse was made a country retreat for members of the Crazy Gang in 1933, when Porchways was built for 'Teddy' Albert Cromwell Knox and wife Clarice Mayne, who were married at East Preston. George Black, agent Horace Reeve, and bandleader Jack Hylton also had homes on the estate, while James Holloway had a residence near Sea Lane House. The Crazy Gang was virtually in residence from 1932 until 1940, and gave performances at village entertainments during the Second World War.[3] George Black had made a fortune from his father's waxworks show and the sale of a chain of cinemas; he then ran the Palladium from 1928 until his death in 1945.

There have been many other celebrities in the two villages, from Sir Maurice Craig, a neurologist of Salona whose 1935 headstone is in the churchyard, to Stanley Holloway with his 1982 memorial.

19

THE GREAT WAR

Sussex has always been in the front line of invasions, 1066 and the Armada being best known. Kingston had a convenient landing stade at the rife in 1587, which may earlier have been a more substantial port.[1] Beacons in the two villages formed part of a relay to warn of invasion.[2] In 1759 crofts by the sea south of both villages were named Watch House, and were probably there to warn of the French not Spanish. In 1801 came the great Napoleonic scare, with plans made for evacuation from the coastal region of men, women and children, farm livestock and vehicles. Even given the small population at that time the logistics were frightening. Besides a number of draught cattle and other animals the two villages had several hundred sheep to be driven over the Downs to the north. Would George Olliver and William Holden have coped as superintendents? Fortunately the test never came and peace prevailed for another hundred years.[3]

The Boer War had its local casualties, but was a prelude to the Great War of 1914:

> My father was the local carrier with horses stabled behind the *Three Crowns*. He had a big roan called Jim and another called Punch. Jim was used as a cab horse and Dad used to come home and change into his driving coat and go and harness up Jim to take out local residents on regular outings in the summer. He worked with his brother-in-law Mr Stoner who was the landlord of the *Lamb Inn*. He joined up with the army in 1915, soon after war broke out, and was killed at Ypres in the spring of 1918.[4]

War in Europe had long been predicted and it was almost with relief that Britain entered the conflict in August 1914. As early as 1909 Major Andrews of Bay Trees was warning of possible invasion, and the need for conscription, in speeches for the National Service League at the schoolroom.

Of those in the two villages who answered the call, Percy Newman was the first to be injured, in September as the German advance was halted; then in November came the first death, of young midshipman Phillip Candy of East Kingston on HMS *Monmouth*, sunk at the Battle

126   *Midshipman Candy, c.1914.*
Philip Candy of East Kingston went down with HMS Monmouth, *1 November 1914.*

127 *Carnival Float, 1907.*
The 'Car of all Nations'.
Frank Standing is the third
figure from the front.

of Coronel off Chile. By now those at home must have begun to realise what the war would bring, as the Army found itself bogged down at Ypres. Percy Newman of Manor Road was the first East Preston loss, in May 1915, during an assault by the Royal Sussex at Neuve Chappelle.

As the years ground by so accounts of battles rolled in with their casualty lists, not only in Europe but also from the Middle East campaign. The USA was finally forced to participate in April 1917, thereby sealing the fate of Germany.

War began with the youngest local victim in Phillip Candy, only 15 years old, and towards the end claimed perhaps the oldest, Frank Standing aged 47. The worst sets of casualties were for the Boxall family, next door to Frank at 1 Louisa Villas, where two sons were lost, one of them in the Canadian Army, and the two Newman sons at Manor Road.

The tragedy of the War has been brought forcibly home to this village by the news of the death of Corporal Percy Newman of the Second Battalion Royal Sussex Regiment who was killed while taking part in the charge at Richebourg l'Avenue on the 9th May. Newman who was

128   *War Memorial Triptych*.
Church war memorial altar, with the Great War triptych, during a flower festival: 'Jesu Mercy In undying Memory of the Officers and Men from this Parish who gave their Lives in the Great War 1914-1918 Faithful Unto Death.'

twenty four years of age and whose home was in Manor Road saw a good deal of fighting in the earlier stages of the war when he had the misfortune to be wounded in the battle of the Aisne. After a brief stay in hospital at Nantes he was invalided home for a few months but left for the Front again on the 6th April. Another son of Mrs Newman is serving with the Fourth Battalion RS.[5]

On 9 April at Richebourg L'Avou:

> The day started with an issue of tea and rum at 3.30am … Bombardment commenced at 5am … The advance over the parapet was made in line … Before our supporting Companies were clear of the first line breastworks the 5th Battalion Royal Sussex arrived, many of them going over the breastworks and becoming mingled with our men … In general the centre of gravity of the assaulting troops did not get much more than 150 yards or about half way to the German Breastworks … one man reached the parapet itself. At 6.30am orders were given to withdraw behind our first breastworks … what remained of the battalion were retired behind the Rue de Bois.

Fourteen officers and 548 men were reported as killed, wounded and missing. 'Our casualties were due to machine gun fire, shrapnel, and high explosive shells, when advancing over the first breastwork.'[6]

War memorials record 22 names, four from Kingston, but it must not be assumed they were all strictly from the two parishes, and at least one lived at West Preston although previously had attended East Preston school. Others are possibly recorded elsewhere, like Captain Norman Kohnstamm of Kingmere, South Strand, and also of Hampstead. Fourteen of the casualties had enlisted before the end of 1915. The church still has its war memorial of 1919,[7] not only a triptych in the south aisle where there had been a small organ, but also the larger memorial organ nearby.[8] A village memorial to two wars, next to the library, was at last promoted by the Royal British Legion and dedicated in 1991. The Kingston memorial was no doubt provided by Mr Candy soon after 1918.

The first vicar of East Preston, E.T. Williams, expressed the Christian attitude to war:

> Christians will loathe and hate it as the work of the devil, and do their very utmost to make War impossible, by changing this bestial economic system of unrestrained competition which makes war inevitable, and by quenching those lusts and passions that lead to War. But they will recognise that when every effort has been made to preserve peace there are circumstances in which God Himself commands them to defend the right and uses a nation as His instrument in the surgical operation on the selfish heart of man.

129   *War Memorial organ, 1986* installed 1919. *Mr E. Bartlett FRCO gave 'an excellent recital'.*

130   *Kingston War Memorial, 2000.*
Great War memorial on the road verge south of East Kingston.

And later he looked forward to the end of the war: 'Grant us all, in His own good time, to meet again and to worship Him round the altar of St Mary's in the little village you all love so well.'[9] Israel Zangwill, the Jewish novelist at Far End, expressed similar sentiments:

> What I really believe is that you should fight with the sword in one hand, and the olive branch in the other, and be always ready to use either. The notion that we can utterly destroy Germany is absolutely absurd to anyone who has read history.[10]

Village families could only wait and do what they could for the war effort, with many normal activities curtailed. Mr W. Hollis' development of Angmering-on-Sea was virtually halted. He did manage to build the club, which was used by members, and also to entertain wounded soldiers and others in the district.[11] But the village became more directly involved in the war effort when the workhouse became a military hospital and Preston Place a POW camp.

31   *The Rev. Williams, before 935. A Calvary to his memory is n the churchyard.*

32   *POW camp nurse, 1918. Watercolour of unknown urse, probably Voluntary Aid Detachment. Signed 'P. Seifert 18', one of the German POWs.*

Preston Place (Hall) had been vacated by the Warren family when R.A. Warren and his wife died in 1911 and 1912, but it was not until 1918 that it was taken over by the military to house German soldiers. An eyewitness in March wrote, 'We all went for a little walk this afternoon after I came home, and we saw some of the prisoners who came here yesterday. We saw a little group of them standing smoking outside the front door up Preston Place, and several walking about the grounds.'[12] The prisoners were extensively employed locally on the farms and nurseries locally, being resolved not to escape and die heroically in the trenches. Lieutenant Coleman, lodging at Sunnyside in Sea Road, took charge with a contingent of the Middlesex Regiment. It was not until October 1919 that the POWs, about 160 men in all, were at last returned to Germany.[13]

The workhouse had been taken over rather earlier, in July 1917, and over 100 soldiers arrived in November.[14] Workhouse patients at the infirmary were sent to Cuckfield workhouse while the children were boarded out at homes in Shoreham. Adjoining the workhouse to the south was Lorne Villa and its large croft, largely orchard, was acquired on lease to provide extra nurses' accommodation. The village library, established there in 1906, was given over to wounded soldiers, and an Entertainments Committee arranged other amusements, and also provided a YMCA hut.[15] It is recalled that the wounded men wore light blue uniforms with white edges, the 'blue coats'. They were a familiar sight in the village:

> Dear Sir – Just a word on behalf of the wounded at Preston. To all concerned at East Preston and outskirts who have done their bit towards the comfort of the Tommies. We all appreciate your kindness and generosity which have been shown to us, and wherever we travel when we leave here we will always think of the happy times we had whilst at East Preston. Yours truly Pte W.P. Gudgeon King's Own R. L. Regt.[16]

By September 1919 the workhouse had been returned to its familiar use.

Comforts for the soldiers were industriously knitted by the Mothers Union and others, who bought wool with the East Preston War Relief Fund. Even the schoolchildren had to lend a hand, and it was recalled how,

133   *POW woodcarving, 2004.*
The top of a small wooden box, now in the USA, with carved emblems. On various sides are the initials C.A. and Josef Bauknecht, Freiburg, Infantry Regiment 185, and the regimental badge for the Middlesex Regiment.

134   *POW British Staff,*
1919.
A group of British soldiers
with their officer, probably
Lieut. G.A. Coleman,
lodging at Sunnyside in Sea
Road.

During the war we had few games, knitting for the war effort instead,
sending scarves and mittens to the men at the Front. We took 6d. a
week for the War Savings although we couldn't really afford it with our
father in the army. The boys had several allotments as War Gardens
next to the school, and grew potatoes and other vegetables, which they
took through the village on carts to sell.[17]

Some quarter of an acre was taken in from the nearby allotments as
this war garden, which the older boys often tended instead of playing
games.

It is notable that the removal of children from London in the Second
World War was presaged by a smaller exodus in 1917. Some eight new
names appeared in the school registers, marked as 'Temporary from
London during the Air Raids'.[18]

135   *POW fistball team,*
1919.
Unknown soldiers at
Preston Place. Security was
lax by some accounts, but
much of their time at the
camp was spent after the
war had ended.

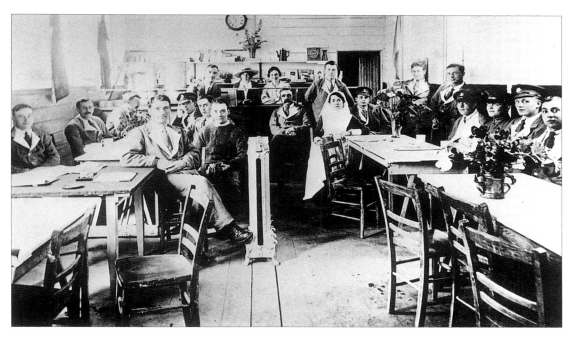

136 *Wounded Soldiers,*
c.1918.
'Blue Coat' wounded
soldiers at the workhouse
military hospital, probably
in the YMCA hut provided.

Food production was a priority and, as most of the parish was still sensibly under crops, the Agricultural Committees had work to do. At West Kingston Mr Beer had to plough up meadows, while in Preston not even Church Field, Langmead's Land today, was sacrosanct: 'The Park connected with Preston Place is one of the many fields throughout the country which has been ploughed up for sowing of corn. The crop of oats, however, grown there this year does not appear to be very successful.'[19] With the sea at hand there was also abundant fishing, with Messrs Booker amongst those thus engaged. This did not prevent food rationing, though, which began in September 1917, and there were even shortages of coal.

It was during this war that many people saw their first aeroplanes; aviators from Shoreham often flew low over the houses and seashore, giving everyone a fright. Others were not so skilled or lucky, a flying officer losing his life after getting lost and crashing when trying to land in Angmering.[20] A USA landing field in West Preston was barely used in 1918.

A similar revolution in land transport was also taking place. As the vast majority of horses sent out to France never returned, motor vehicles became ascendant. Local main roads were tarred in 1916. It was now that Mr Stoner of Rustington went over to taxis, and his daughter was one of the first lady cabbies. At South Strand in 1917, Edwin Goode had his 'little red bus' running through Patching to Worthing, a Biaco based on a Ford car chassis. It was only after 1919 that Southdown became dominant.

The great flu epidemic of 1918 closed the school more than once, but at long last peace could be celebrated: 'The children were assembled in the main room and sang the National Anthem. Cheers were then given for the King and our soldiers and sailors who have won such a great victory.'[21] On 19 July 1919 the village, in common with others across the land, held its Peace Celebrations. These included a procession nearly half a mile long, with decorated cars and bicycles, sports and a comic cricket match in the recreation ground, tug-of-war, children's tea in the barn, concert and, finally, a grand firework display.[22]

137   *Horse cab*, c.1910. *One of the horse cabs belonging to Arthur Stoner of Rustington.*

20

The Second World War

For a time the 'piece of paper' was applauded. 'By his initiative, foresight, courage, and sanctified common-sense he has saved the world from war,' wrote the vicar.[1] But county plans for civil defence had been under way since 1935, and in 1936 Major Smithers was made the village ARP officer with a deputy.[2] In 1938 ARP Wardens were in place, and by 1939 private air-raid shelters were being built. A warning siren at the workhouse was superseded by one at the fire station which came into operation, at the barn in North Lane, during April 1940. Its first officer was Mr C.G. Smith.

At first the locality was considered safe enough for evacuees from London, who began pouring into country villages after Germany invaded Poland in September 1939. A teacher from Tooting was taken away from his charges in Littlehampton and, with another teacher, took classes of refugees in the YMCA schoolroom, some sixty children in addition to ninety villagers at the combined schools. By the end of the year only twenty were left, many moving away when invasion of the south coast seemed imminent.

School log-books constantly reported dog-fights as the Battle of Britain was fought overhead. Drills with gas masks took place in case of bombing, but fortunately the only serious incident affecting the village took place on 10 July 1940, when four bombs were dropped on East Preston Nursery in Vermont Drive. Two men were killed and others injured, John Marpole having his name placed on the church triptych next to servicemen who lost their lives.[3] Probably the best thing the school got out of the war was the provision of good dinners at the nearby Conservative Hall from November 1943.[4]

L.M. Gander, writing in 1945, recalled the situation after Dunkirk:

Adults and children alike found plenty of excitement and interest in our village, which was soon buzzing with military activity. Coldstream Guards back from France, hurriedly and only partially re-equipped, were sent to take over this stretch of the coast, and soldiers and civilians were, for a time, mixed in the oddest way. My wife, Hilda, and I set out one day to sunbathe on the beach, and she asked whether I would

138   Bomb crater, 1940. Bomb crater and greenhouse damage at Frampton's Nursery in Vermont Drive, July 1940.

prefer the machine-gun beach or the anti-tank section … I went to the headquarters of the Local Defence Volunteers situated in a ramshackle rifle-range. At that time the force, afterwards called the Home Guard, were popularly known as 'Parashots', because their chief function was supposed to be stalking enemy parachutists. I offered my services as a week-end soldier was allowed to sign a form, and told I might begin rifle practice when enrolment was approved by 'Arundel', whatever that meant. I was also shown a rack of some twenty old Lee Enfield rifles, our total armament, and told that there were about fifteen uniforms among 150 volunteers.[5]

Capt. Revel was in command of the East Preston and Kingston Home Guard until 1941, when it was taken over by Capt. Girling, and finally by Lt Barnard in 1943. The rifle range where they trained is today the Warren Room of the Village Hall.

As part of the defence against invasion, in 1940 gun batteries were located along the coast. At Bognor were two 5½in guns and at Worthing two 6in guns, and the only battery between them was a 6in gun in East Preston, at the end of the Pergolas garden, South Strand. Smaller concrete pill-boxes in East Preston and Kingston were for machine guns, the last of these at Kingston being demolished in 1973.[6] A searchlight unit occupied the meadow west of East Kingston farmstead.

From the autumn of 1941 until after D-Day our defence largely fell into the hands of Canadian forces: early on the French Canadians and, at the end of the war, a battalion of the 15th Canadian Recc. Regt. On 18 August 1942 the Canadians took part in the infamous Dieppe raid, and of those involved half were either casualties or captured.

Apart from the rifle range used by the Home Guard, various facilities in the cricket ground were taken over by the Forces. These included the YMCA, north of the present play area, from July 1940, after it was vacated by the evacuee school. A number of entertainments were staged there over the next few years by the voluntary services. Local entertainers mentioned in one performance included Clarice Mayne, Hilda Munday, Billy Carroll and Nervo and Knox. Towards the end of the war, when the situation was more relaxed, the Canadians entertained the village with three days of sports, racing, jumping, tug-of-war, and their band playing. The barn was finally derequisitioned in June 1946, when the war in Europe was over.

As the threat of invasion in 1940 receded, precautions improved, from the building of air-raid shelters to the construction of a line of concrete-block tank traps along the greensward and beach and tubular iron structures in the sea to frustrate landing craft. The immediate coastal strip was restricted, except to inquisitive small boys, and many of the houses were requisitioned for military use.

Members of a Scottish regiment were stationed at Kingston before D-Day and recall how,

> Houses built expensively for those who could afford seaside holiday homes became the unit's billets. Part of A Squadron, occupying the house of a famous man of theatres at Kingston Gorse [George Black, owner of the Palladium], lived among stained glass, a shining cocktail bar, sunken baths and garden fountains. Other people of the stage whose homes were here became the regiment's friends, notably Nervo and Knox, who renewed old acquaintance months latter, when they were making the Second Army laugh in Holland.

Final training included a ramble in the countryside, 'four days marched by squadrons eighty miles over the Sussex Downs, finishing with a forced march back to Amberley'. Shortly afterwards they were part of the invasion force, many of them on a one-way ticket.[7]

The Women's Institute, Auxiliary, and Voluntary Service, were the principal female organisations, apart from the Red Cross. Miss Scott of Greencroft in Sea Lane, for instance, was not only the president of the WI but also an ARP driver who attended the local HQ every evening.

139 *Pergolas, c.1930, owned by William Hollis. A Second World War naval gun was sited at the south end of The Lawns path, in the foreground.*

Greencroft is also recalled as the village centre for canning produce for the winter. Both the WVS and the Women's Auxiliary did great service in the village, running canteens for the forces.

What was originally Ferring Detachment of the Red Cross, formed in 1939 under Commandant S. Barker of Ferring, then under Mr Mackenzie Ross of Golden Acre, became an East Preston group with its headquarters at Roundstone Drive, next to the fire station. Various members assisted at the workhouse during its use as an emergency hospital, when many evacuees from London hospitals were lodged there. Exercises were held at Mount Roland, Sea Lane, which was a school but is now apartments known as Angmering Court. Members attended casualties including those wounded in the East Preston Nursery raid.[8] Another detachment, not established until 1943, was mainly for young women. Their HQ was at one of the North Lane Cottages where there are now shops.

Even before the end of the war some wounded members of the forces were being welcomed home after long periods of captivity, their release negotiated by the Red Cross. These included Sgt Megenis of Manor Road, captured before Dunkirk, who then spent over three years as a POW. For most of the Forces, return to civilian life did not take place until 1946. The British Legion and Parish Council organised a Welcome Home Coming.

Formal victory celebrations were pre-empted in August 1945 by the residents of Somerset Road, Half Moon Road (north of Roundstone Crossing) and Roundstone, with a street party for eighty children and sports. It concluded with a bonfire and dancing for the adults. But the formal Victory Day was 8 June 1946 and involved the whole village. Sports in the cricket field were followed by tea for 200 children, but for the adults there would be a simple religious service, conducted by the Rev. Fincham and the Rev. Mudie Draper, and playing of hymns. The Rev. Fincham expressed his feelings in 1945:

> We have been giving thanks that, so far as Europe is concerned, the war is over. That the maiming and killing of fellow human beings has come to an end; that a bad system of government has been broken; and that a theory of aggression has come to grief in its own rottenness, are things for which we are all truly thankful. As Christians we do not rejoice because of the suffering inflicted on the common people in enemy lands ... [9]

The war memorial outside the library records the names of 20 men and women of the Armed Forces and other services who died in the conflict. At the church an earlier book of remembrance also included the civilian killed at East Preston Nursery. J.E. Gordon of Kingston Manor was another who died.[10] Unlike those killed in the First World War, several were buried in local churchyards.[11] Others are abroad, from South Africa to Burma.

140   *J. Eschbaecher, 1941, of Baytree Cottage, in Red Cross uniform.*

Social Life

Recreation and sports before the 19th century were enjoyed within the round of religious and farming festival. Organised sports and social clubs were a phenomenon of the Victorian era. Parish magazines of 1902 and later reveal how recreational clubs must have proliferated. The school was the village hall of that time, hosting slide and cinema lectures, concerts by children and the glee choir, evening classes in wood carving and drawing, mothers' meetings, missionary society and Sunday school. There were clothing and other charitable and savings clubs, whist and cribbage at the reading room, a parish library, cricket, football, quoits and village sports, harvest homecoming celebrations at Preston Place and harvest festivals at the church, not to mention the workhouse, with its outings and concerts, and coronation and other national festivities as they happened.

The church choir was at its peak after 1872 when a choir festival was held annually in the district. On at least one occasion the bishop was present when the event was held at Arundel church.[1] The choir had yearly train trips to London and elsewhere. It must be imagined how those who frequented the beer shop and inn entertained themselves singing old ballads and folk songs.[2]

An inkling of old customs is found in 1893 when the schoolmaster reported, 'At least a dozen children are absent, they have gone round with garlands of flowers, Maying, as they call it.' Only later did the school encourage garland day, folk song and dance. Tipteers or Mummers Plays, revived and rearranged in the years around 1900, were a pale reflection of an old tradition. Charles Barnard lived at Slater's Cottages until his death in 1899, and found it lucrative to take a band of boys round the village at Christmas, acting the Mummers Play, but it is uncertain where he had obtained his version. Later, in

141 *Boating on East Kingston pond, 1917.*
Children had little need for organised games. Ivo Candy with his dog Peter on the pond at East Kingston, 1917.

1911, Alfred Foard of the same cottages revived this custom. Finally, in 1913, Richard Sharp, a solicitor living at Kingmere (South Strand) from about 1910, expanded the East Preston version, and eventually performances were staged at hotels in Brighton and elsewhere.[3]

> In comes I, Old Father Christmas; am I welcome or am I not?
> I hope Old Father Christmas will never be forgot.

In the same year he also helped form the Folk Dance or East Preston Morris Dance troupe, which had its brief life in that pre-war age of old English romanticism, folksong collecting and revivals. He returned from war service in the RND and moved to Chichester, taking the Tipteers Play with him to adapt, and set up the Boxgrove Mummers in 1927. He died in 1953.

142   *Folk Dance troupe, 1914.*

Morris Dancers in the Cricket Field. Richard Sharpe is seated third from the left.

The Stickleback Pierrot troupe, managed by Mr Hennell from 1906 until he left the village, was another folksy fancy of the era.

❊ ❊ ❊

Cricket is an ancient game that made the Beehives croft and barn the centre of village festivity from the late 19th century onwards. It was played locally by the mid-century, and no doubt earlier on particular occasions. In 1856 the end of the Crimean War was marked by celebrations in fields belonging to Preston Place, when local villages played matches against each other. At a purely social occasion in West Kingston, George Olliver staged a match between sides representing Ferring and Kingston, although small villages often banded together to create a team and East Preston men on his estate probably supplemented Kingston players. Similarly, at

144 *Blaauw Cup detail.* 'East Preston Cricket League Blaauw Challenge Cup. May 2 1900'.

143 *Cricket Club team, 1900.*

The cricket club history provides names for these village characters, many of whom are mentioned in these pages. Top row: F. Challen, Mr Sturtevant, the workhouse master, Arthur Charman of Beehive Cottages, R. Ayling of Boxtree Cottages, George Biles, retired coastguard officer and recreation ground superintendent, then of Louisa Villas. Centre row: C. Sturtevant, C.E. Challen, then at the Three Crowns, *H.L. Havers of the Norris Nursery, A. Foard, Albert Booker jnr, then of Manor Road. Seated: Mr Blaauw, nurseryman and donator of the League Cup, then lodging at Vine Cottages, H. Mills, and Henry Roberts of the Elm Cottage family, later a county cricketer. The only significant person missing is the cup-winning captain, F.B. O'Neill of Vine Cottages.*

harvest homes in September, a dinner at a farm such as the Homestead would be followed by amusements including cricket.

The date at which formal cricket clubs were formed is uncertain, but fixture cards of the 1920s, for East Preston, contain the testimony 'Founded 1860', which is entirely feasible.[4] But although Ham Park is often mentioned in reports as a venue for matches with Angmering, no ground is named for games at Preston. The present Sea Road recreation ground may already have been in use, after removing the sheep, being a meadow called Green Croft on the Olliver estate at the time.

Club matches involving East Preston were reported from 1868, with games against neighbours such as Ferring. Before the modern weekend it mattered little on which day such events took place, although Sunday was sacred. Mondays, Tuesdays and Fridays were favoured, but for no obvious reason. A feature of the matches was that they had two innings, and 30 in each was a potential winning score.

Prior to 1896 the cricket club in East Preston was not very strong, but in that year a boost was provided when Mr P.W. Nind offered a Challenge Cup to be played for by a village league.[5] Thereupon, at the club AGM, East Preston Cricket League was created including Angmering, Lyminster, Rustington, Ferring, Goring, and Clapham with Patching. The village club immediately came to life, improving its ground with help from the Parish Council, and many more members were recruited. Eventually Goring, a much larger village, dominated, and won possession of the cup in 1899 after three straight wins. In 1900 a new cup was presented by Mr St Leger Blaauw and played for until the outbreak of the First World War, when many old customs came to an end. Preston won this

145   *Cricket Club with Blaauw Cup, 1908.*
East Preston won the cup for the fourth time in 1908. At this time the team included several members of the Norrell family including the captain shown holding the cup. George Biles, umpire, stands to the left.

146   *Warren Cricket Pavilion and Bowling Green, 1965.*
To the right is the old bowling green at the end of its days. The thatched Warren Pavilion is next to the new clubhouse, which has also been replaced.

cup half a dozen times, and the cup itself survives in the ownership of the club.[6] In recent years a knock-out tournament once more played for the cup.

Halcyon days came again with the support of local celebrities after the Second World War. For several years from 1946 charity matches were played against teams of county cricketers and were immensely popular, filling the small ground with several thousand spectators.

An excellent thatched hut was given to the club by the Rev. Warren in 1927, and this served until 1951 when it was moved and another clubhouse built alongside, where an elm rookery had been cleared. The Warren hut was burnt down in 1971.

* * *

The modern annual fancy dress parade continues a much older event bound up with the health and welfare of ordinary villagers. These early carnival parades were organised by the Ancient Order of Foresters, a

147   *Carnival float, 1906. 'Flowers of Preston' carnival float at North Lane. Lily Hills, aged 14, is identified as the central flower.*

friendly society, the local branch of which was founded in 1862 at the *Lamb Inn*, Rustington. Collections were made for local hospitals at a time when there was no National Health Service.

A more ambitious parade got going in 1906 through both East Preston and Rustington. Horse-drawn carts staged tableaux representing the Flowers of Preston and many other themes, accompanied by village bands. This was a yearly event until 1913, not resuming until 1921 apart from the peace pageant of 1919, but then it only continued for a few more years. Modern versions took place in 1977 for the Silver Jubilee, and in 1978 when the village was twinned with Brou, a town south of Chartres in France. But it was in 1982 that the current series of carnival parades began, in conjunction with Festival Week, originally to raise money for church building funds.

* * *

Stoolball is a peculiarly southern English game which still thrives, supposedly originating with milking stools. At the village school in the 19th century sport was for boys, and school cricket was introduced in 1890, but it was not until perhaps 1919 that girls began playing stoolball. A village club was formed before 1916 and possibly as early as 1910, but there are few records. Although cricket was suspended during the war the ladies were able to continue. In 1925 and later the club competed for and won the Orme Cup. The Rev. Orme had been rector of Angmering until he retired to Baytree House in 1913, and his daughters founded the village Girl Guides.

> Major William Grantham J.P. revived the ancient game at auxiliary hospitals in Sussex in 1917-18. In July 1918 East Preston Ladies defeated the Pavilion Blues by scoring 137 to 70 runs at Brighton. [Military Hospital][7]

* * *

148   Carnival float, 1906. 'Pack of Cards'. Mr Sturtevant, on horseback, is the workhouse master; those to the left are believed to be Miss Sturtevant, Miss Warr, Miss Win Corney, and Walter Booker behind.

149   *Stoolball club team,*
1935.
East Preston team that won
the Orme Cup.

Football was evidently played in early days, but as yet there is no knowledge of it before 1908 when the parish magazine reported that a club had been re-formed, with 26 senior and 19 junior members. R.A. Warren was naturally the President. Football was certainly played at school before that. Between the wars the club was in the Worthing District League, and in 1928 won the Croshaw Cup.

Meadows had to be made use of as available, particularly a field by Roundstone Crossing tenanted by dairymen Messrs Roberts. The club had use of a large hut there belonging to Temple Church. A permanent football ground was needed and in 1935 Town Planning set aside land at Lashmar Field for recreation. Then in 1937 the RDC purchased 33 acres for housing, including the 10 acres requested by the Parish Council for recreation and football, three of which became a new school.

Again, the intervention of war resulted in land being taken over for cultivation. It was not until 1946 that it was released and the club was refounded, moving to the recreation ground after it was finally prepared in 1951. Major J.E. Gordon, of Kingston Manor, had donated £500 to the George V fund for playing fields, and this was used towards laying out the field.[8] The new primary school occupied part of this land from 1951.

* * *

Apart from the cricket and football fields, the only other recreation ground in East Preston is Church Field, now named Langmead's Land, conveyed by Mr Langmead to the RDC in 1962.[9] Then, in 1973, Mrs Sharpus of Preston Hall gave the wooded area south of her house as an extension to the grounds. This whole area had been parkland attached to the mansion.[10]

One of the most unfortunate 'natural' changes to the character of the cricket ground and village was the outbreak of elm disease in 1973. All the mature trees were affected and felled. Those seen today are

sucklings, regularly reinfected. The October 1987 hurricane damaged village roofs and felled several trees, but by then there were few elms remaining – a small mercy.

* * *

The founding of the YMCA, or Red Triangle Institute, in East Preston was probably the most important social event of the 20th century. Under the patronage of Messrs Warren it was in charge of recreational facilities, encouraging the formation of a number of clubs, some of which are still with us today. Its facilities were superior to those of the present village hall but the site is now occupied by houses. The church provided First World War memorials, but not the village as such, and this may have stimulated Reginald Warren – a son of R.A. Warren – to move a large timber YMCA hut from Shoreham to the cricket field in 1919. At 80 feet long, it provided a hall with a stage and rooms behind, with a reading room at the east end, and kitchens on the north side.[11]

A report of the 1924 AGM indicates its interests. Membership stood at two hundred.

> The Sunday services had continued to fill a useful place … The entertainment programme had been maintained in a series of concerts, lectures, socials etc … Hospitality was given to the Cricket Club and

150 Football Club team and YMCA hut, 1922. Names are thought to be, top: A.H. Jeffries, YMCA secretary, Charles Bennett, George Cox, Albert Frost, A.A. Seymour. Centre: Albert Greenyer, Harry Boxall, Albert Cox, Ben Larby, Ted Cox. Front: Bill Horne, Doug Middleton, with football, Frank Howick.

151 *Pierrot troupe, 1907.*
'Sticklebacks', a transitory
troupe of pierrots formed
by F.G. Hennell, seated
centre, in 1906. Back: F.
Bennett, A. Challen, W.
Baker, T. Norrell, Mr
Bennett. Centre: A. Norrell,
H. Roberts, B. Larby, F.G.
Hennell, D. Newman, W.
Booker, F. Norrell. Front:
Bob Hawtree.

152 *Church organ, before
1919.*
The first organ at East
Preston church, where the
triptych is at present, was a
small instrument probably
made by Bevington. Before
the 1880s a barrel organ
may have been used to
accompany the choir and
congregation.

153 *YMCA gymnasts,
c.1920s.*
Girls performing
gymnastics in front of the
stage at the institute hut.

154   Bowls and Cricket, 1961.
Bowls and cricket clubs in action when games on Sunday was becoming acceptable. The field is surrounded by ancient elm trees and not the present Norway and American maples.

155   Flower Show, before 1958.
Prize giving at East Preston Flower Show, with A.A. Seymour at the table.

156   Flower Show, 1978.
After being held at the school for a few years the Flower Show returned to the cricket field, or Warren Recreation Ground, for the supposed 50th show – not the 50th year. A marquee was used as in former years.

157   Guides in Cricket Field, after 1922.
1st East Preston Guides soon after being established, under the captaincy of Miss Agnes Wyatt of Rustington Hall, seated third from left. Two patrols were named Robins and Wrens.

158   Barn gymnasium, after 1931.
Mr Ovett of Worthing was the instructor.

159   Scout HQ opening, 1990.
Andi Landon, a Queen's Scout, opening the new Scout HQ, June 1990.

to the Stoolball Club for teas. The Football Club had made excellent headway ... Scouts, Guides and Wolf Cubs were making progress ... the Sports Fete Committee held a very successful meeting on Easter Monday ... The Bowling Club came into existence during the year ... The Committee felt deeply indebted to the President for his handsome gift of the gymnasium ... Thanks were also due to Mr Fairbanks for the badminton sets ... The Horticultural Society were responsible for a successful show and bazaar in the summer and after making a donation of £70 to the funds of the Institute have added to their reserve ... Sir Arthur Yapp [General Secretary of the YMCA] said ... 'he did not know any other village hut in the country so well equipped as that at East Preston'.

160   *Barn and Flower Show, 1983, before alteration to the present Village Hall. Gymnastic apparatus on the walls had been removed several years previously. Some original roof trusses remained.*

Between 1923 and 1931 a cinema programme began at the YMCA, showing many of the silent movies of the era, with Harold Lloyd, Dorothy Gish, and others. Magic Circle entertainments, and dances, took place, and billiard tables were installed in 1923 and matches played.

The arrival of London evacuees in the village necessitated the use of the hut for school classes and brought the normal activities of the YMCA to a sudden end. Within a year most of them had gone, and in July 1940 the hut became a canteen for occupying forces.

In 1945 the YMCA was taken over as a youth centre, but in 1966 it was sold by the Association and later demolished. A few years later, in 1972, the club found excellent new facilities, when the pyramid building opened at the Lashmar Road school. The rest of the cricket field and barn had been given to the Parish Council when the Rev. Warren died in 1942, but not the YMCA.

* * *

The first offshoot of the YMCA was perhaps the Horticultural Society, its first flower show being held in 1920 although discussions had begun years before. Locally, the Clapham and Patching show had begun about 1887. The great marquee and sports in the cricket field were its special features for the next fifty years.

Scouts and Guides groups were formed in 1922,[12] the Guides initially under the leadership of Miss Agnes Wyatt of Rustington Hall.[13] Mr Harold Jeffries of South Norris was GSM for the Scouts in its early days, but after some difficulties the Scout group was reformed in 1931. The venue for meetings was the Reading Room at the east end of Vicarage Lane. This large hut had originally been provided by Admiral Warren in 1913, to replace a room in the Manor House.[14] It was used by various social clubs before the YMCA and other facilities existed. In 1947 Leslie Warren, son of Bernard of Natal, gave the hut to the Association: 'The Warren Hut presented to the Arundel and Littlehampton Boy Scouts Association by L.R. Warren Esq 1947.' This continued in use until 1989, when land was leased from the District Council and the present large hall was built on the recreation ground south of Preston Place. A cottage called 'Baden' is on the site today. The Guides found new quarters at Lashmar Recreation Ground.

The parish had its own library early, from 1906, but it was in 1927 that a county library was established at the YMCA, moving from behind the stage to the other end later. It was not until 1962 that the present library was built in the Street, being extended in 1984.[15]

In 1923 the bowling club was founded, using a green to the west of the YMCA until 1967, when the present grounds were opened by the Duchess of Norfolk. R.O. Warren, Sir Maurice Craig, and R.N. Fairbanks presided in the early days, with championship cups provided by Mr Candy and others. This new ground was given to the Parish Council by Helen Gordon, of the adjoining house Bydand (Seaview) and the Kingston Manor family, in 1936, but war delayed use of it other than for garden allotments.

Another sports facility created during 1924 was the hard tennis court in the field next to the cricket ground. By September matches were being played there, including a tournament for the boys of the Siamese School at Rustington. Nowadays it can be hired for casual use.

* * *

Stables adjoined the cricket field barn, and were used by Messrs Roberts' dairymen as cow stalls in 1917.[16] In 1931 the widow of Reginald Warren converted them to a rifle range, with a new brick part at the west end.[17] Between 1933 and 1951 the range was administered by trustees, who gave it to the Parish Council, although the club continued until 1960.[18] From 1967 it was used by the Evangelical Free Church, but after considerable alteration was finally opened in 1981 as the first stage of the village hall.

Already in occasional use by the village, the cricket field barn was converted in 1923 by Reginald Warren to a gymnasium and badminton court, with a 'fives' court, or general ball games area, adjoining. In 1942 it was included in the cricket field bequest to the Parish Council, for the benefit of the village, by his brother, the Rev. Warren.[19] Proposals from 1945 onwards for a British Legion hall were not agreed, and a public meeting rejected a draft scheme for a war memorial hall, and so the

161   *Bowling Green, after 1923.*
A bowls match at the old green, probably several years after it was established in 1923. The YMCA is behind.

former barn was leased to Clifford Smith, an estate agent, as an auction room. A village hall committee sat from 1961 onwards, and after the YMCA closed an excellent scheme for a youth club at the barn in 1971 was not considered suitable. Renewed interest did finally bring agreement and, following the 1981 first stage, the barn opened as the second stage of the village hall in 1984. It should not be forgotten that in 1931 Mrs R. Warren donated £1,000 as the Warren Trust to finance the YMCA, and afterwards a village hall, which helped fund that eventual scheme.

* * *

The former Temple Choir hut, now in Vicarage Lane, became the 1931 venue for the first Women's Institute in East Preston, founded at the instigation of Mrs Paget, the churchwarden's wife.[20] A nursing home now occupies part of this site. At the first WI meeting on 13 June 1931 there were 40 members, and the vicar's wife Mrs Willams was president. Then, as numbers grew and new accommodation was needed, a move

162   *View from Workhouse, 1969.*
View from top floor of the workhouse, with the library left, Forge House far right, and Highdown in the distance.

163   *Tennis Exhibition
Match, 1936.*
*'H.W. Austin and Dr
Prenn at the South-West
Sussex Lawn Tennis Club'
celebrate the club re-
opening on 22 August.*

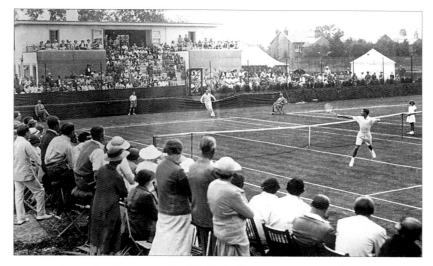

was made to the Conservative Hall, built in 1928 on land given by Mrs
Gordon of Kingston, and evidently financed by H. Aron of the Bungalow,
Angmering-on-Sea, as the foundation stone used to proclaim.[21]

Tennis was a game that became popular with the affluent people who
came to live at South Strand after the club and its grounds were laid out
by Mr Hollis. Grass courts were prepared by 1914, and a tournament
in 1916 and open tournaments in 1917 were the first held.[22] The war
brought a temporary halt until 1920, when six new courts became
available south of the *Willowhayne Hotel*, on what since 1960 has been
the Village Green. Well known players took part, such as Mr M.J.G.
Ritchie and A.A. Fyzee from India.

The final move began in 1929 with the laying of 12 grass courts at
Homelands Avenue, the last tournament at Willowhayne taking place
in 1930. The foundation stone of the new clubhouse was laid in 1930
by the local MP, and the Duke of Norfolk was president. The sale of
Angmering-on-Sea by Mr Hollis in 1932 no doubt caused the dissolution
of the Sports Club Syndicate, but in 1935 the newly created Ratepayers
Association revived it as the South West Lawn Tennis Club. Yet another
clubhouse was built and opened that year but later became the private
house Lismore.[23] In 1936 an exhibition game took place between Mr
H. (Bunny) Austin, the Davis Cup player, and D.R. Prenn, which Austin
won.

Once again war intervened and the grounds were abandoned, the
clubhouse becoming a vandalised ruin. In 1948 the new owner, H.L.
Smith, finally conveyed part of the grounds to East Preston Parish Council
and, despite several offers to purchase, it has remained in their hands.
The East Preston Lawn Tennis Club has leased the grounds since that
time, although they are now hard courts.

164 *Bulb Fields*, c.1915.
Bulb fields west of Sea Lane. Mr Waghorn, the manager of Oakley Lodge, is to the extreme right. The Willowhayne estate occupies these fields today. The flowers were sent to market in London.

FROM VILLAGE TO MILLENNIUM

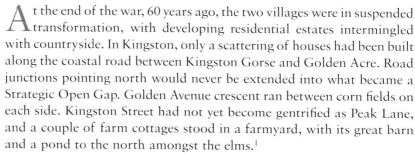

At the end of the war, 60 years ago, the two villages were in suspended transformation, with developing residential estates intermingled with countryside. In Kingston, only a scattering of houses had been built along the coastal road between Kingston Gorse and Golden Acre. Road junctions pointing north would never be extended into what became a Strategic Open Gap. Golden Avenue crescent ran between corn fields on each side. Kingston Street had not yet become gentrified as Peak Lane, and a couple of farm cottages stood in a farmyard, with its great barn and a pond to the north amongst the elms.[1]

In East Preston, development had yet to vault the barrier of the railway, to the north of which was Half Moon Nursery. Other glasshouse nurseries surrounded North Lane, including Norris Nursery and Shenfield, built in 1899 for Mr Havers, and there were extensive orchards where Orchard Drive is today.[2] East Preston Nurseries in Vermont Drive was the last to go, in 1975, after which The Framptons estate replaced it, Vermont House now no longer surrounded by cornfields. Only Graperies Nursery had been demolished before the war, leaving much of its land derelict and bramble-grown, brick water tanks full of newts and frogs, a playground for young children.

Willowhayne estate had a few substantial houses along Tamarisk Way and in The Ridings, but otherwise open fields continued far into West Preston, past Pigeonhouse Lane. North from that extended the meadows near the church and Church Field, all scheduled to be public open space, although the meadows were eventually lost. Lashmar Field was also a scheduled open space, with the school site next to it. The only other spaces set aside were the future village green in Sea Road, Homelands tennis courts and, of course, the long established cricket field and bowling green site, surrounded by ancient elm trees. In Sea Road the field to the north of the Homestead was occupied by Mr Wright, as his smallholding, and by the school were allotments where shops would be built five years after the school closed.

Main roads in the village, together with the Roundstone bypass, A259, were just old country lanes with hedgerows and elms bordering them,

165 *The Street, early 20th century.*
View south from near Preston Place, its grounds to the right. Fields and hedgerows predate housing development in the 1920s.

only surfaced in the early years of the century. Sea Lane in particular was shaded by large elms trees along its whole length. For another generation yet, there were fewer cars on Roundstone bypass than are to be encountered today in the village. Walking was enjoyable and a group could cross the A259 in safety, holding up few cars. The proposed inter-village road still threatened the area through Vicarage Lane and North Lane, but long delay brought its abandonment.

Since that time the story has been the rapid infilling of houses, both in the village and north to Angmering. In the early 21st century all that is left of open fields are the regulation recreation grounds, with no open spaces for new social facilities. The former workhouse nurses' home, Martlets, is likely to be rebuilt and part of it was proposed for a parish room. Whereas primary development on open land was at fairly low density, creating a garden village, any builder now must first demolish, which can only be made economical by erecting flats and densely packed housing, rendering the village a mere extension of 'Worthinghampton'. Local planning effort to preserve the character of Sussex, in an increasingly overpopulated county, is a difficult task.

166 *Sea Lane floods, 1974.*
Autumn floods in Sea Lane inundated some houses.

Appendix 1

Rentals, Surveys, Land Tax and Inventory

East Preston 1602 Rental

Preston Rents there per annum 1602

Leases	Rich. Parker farmor there	£8	10s.	
	Edward Gawen farmor there		53s.	4d.
Copiholders	Wm. Parker jun.		10s.	
	Phillippe Pococke		14s.	
	Robert Martyn		26s.	8d.
	Robert Master		6s.	
	Johane Hamon Wydd		22s.	
	Elizabeth Whittington Wydd		22s.	
	Johane Gawen Wydd		15s.	
	John Ede		17s.	
	John Smythe		18s.	
	Wm. Parker sen.		17s.	
	Phillippe Stamer		2s.	
	Eden Parker Wydd		1s.	
Summa		£19	14s.	
Quytt rentes	John Younge for Reedes landes		9s.	7d.
	Wm. Parker sen for Wm. Fuller als Harris for landes there		1s.	4d.
	Rich. Parker for landes late Mr Rich. Threeles [of Loxwoodd] there		2s.	1d.
	John Ede for Phillippe Gratwickes landes deceased		1s.	8d.
	Tho. Mathew for the said Gratwickes lande		1s.	8d.
	John Lenne of Weeke sen. for the landes of Thomas Grene deceased		1s.	11d.
	Thomas Grene of Upmarden for landes called [blank]		2s.	9d.

The rental has no total valuation for the manor, but the following amounts may be calculated:

Lease for the farm	£8	10s.	0d.
do	£2	13s.	4d.
Copyholds	£8	10s.	8d.
Quit rent freeholds	£1	1s.	0d.
TOTAL	£20	15s.	0d.

1602

Kingeston Rentes there per annum 1602

Leases in Kingeston	The Farme there per annum			£14	2s.
	Kingeston wyndemyll per annum			£4	
	The Farme also payeth yearely	Wheate x qtrs	10 qtrs		
		Barly x qtrs	10 qtrs		
	Summa			£18	2s.
Copiholders	John Grene als Smythe				24s.
	Wm. Springe				8s.

Edward Wattes			6s.
Rich Knight in Jur uxor			14s. 7d.
John Easted			14s. 3d.
Wm. Springe jun.			21s.
Henry Ede			[?]
John Springe			[23s. 3d.]
Robert Wylkyn			[blank]
Edward Drewett			[13s.]
John Grene als Smythe jun.			[18s. 3d.]
John Symes			[?]
Agnes Stamer Wydd			[39s. 7d.]
John Locke			3s. 4d.
Cotages buylte	Morris Pannett		1s.
John Graye			1s.
Rich Stapler			1s.
Rich Tyckenor			1s.
Thomas Myllard			6d.
Robert Pannett jun.			6d.
Robert Pannett sen.			6d.

Quytt rentes Thomas Trewelove of Preston for landes late
Henry Mychelborne of Arondell gent.

[& sometyme Frannces Dawtrey esquyer] per annum	16s.
Wm. Springe for landes late Rich Gawens deceased	5d.
Wm. Wolvyn of Feringe for a Ten't & v	
acres of landes in Kingeston	1s. 2d.
[blank] Hills of Billyngeshurste for [5 acres] landes	
there called [blank]	1s. 2d.

The rental has no total valuation for the manor, but the following amounts may be calculated:

Lease for the farm	£14 2s. 0d.
Lease for the windmill	£4 0s. 0d.
Copyholds	£13 3s. 7d.
Cottages	5s. 6d.
Quit rent freeholds	18s. 9d.
TOTAL	£32 9s. 10d.

The three copyholds for which rents are not individually known total £4 3s. 10d., indicating at least one large holding.

1671 Survey or Terrier

East Preston

Leaseholds		Traditional areas
Sotcher	£70 rising to £75 rent per annum for 9 years from 1671	168 acres

The three leaseholds following were all formerly copyholds for lives

Whittington	22s. rent for 99 years or for lives from 1671	23 acres
Cook	10s. rent for 99 years or lives from 1671	8 acres
Laurence	£19 rent for 21 years from 1656	34 acres

Freeholds paying quit rent

Cook	6s. quit rent per annum	61 acres
Cook	2s. 1d. quit rent	8 acres
Holden	1s. 6d. quit rent	12 acres
Grattwicke	1s. 8d. quit rent	4 acres
Baker	1s. 4d. quit rent	8 acres
Martin	1s. 8d. quit rent	10 acres

Copyholds for lives

Martin	24s. rent	from 1653	22 acres
Martin	2s. 8d. rent	from 1653	2 acres
Martin	14s. rent	from 1656	7 acres
Lydgater	15s. rent	from 1653	12 acres
Masters	6s. rent	from 1662	3½ acres

Not in survey book

Weeks	freehold and not paying quit rent	
Green	freehold	do
Evans	freehold	do

Glebe and some minor freeholds not in the survey

Kingston Tenants 1671

Leasehold

			Traditional areas
Pannet	£100 per annum for 21 years	from c.1650	174 acres

Leaseholds formerly copyholds for lives

Baker	£40 rent for 21 years	from 1663	15 acres
Wright	£40 rent for 21 years	from 1670	82 acres
do	£5 10s. rent for yearly lease		10 acres
Laurence	£5 rent for 21 years	from 1656	12 acres
Heberden	£6 rent for yearly lease		13 acres
Oulder	£10 rent for 21 years	from 1656	20 acres

Freeholds paying quit rents

Oulder	2s. 4d. quit rent	8 acres
Wright	5d. quit rent	3½ acres
Elphick	16s. quit rent	57 acres

Copyholds of Inheritance (virtual freeholds)

Drewett	13s. rent	from 1662	10 acres
Oliver	3s. 4d. rent	from 1659	2½ acres
Bennett	14s. 3d. rent	from 1659	12 acres
do	8s. 6d. rent	from 1659	8 acres
Oulder	17s. 4d. rent	from 1653	15 acres
do	16s. 6d. rent	from 1653	12 acres
do	3s. rent	from 1653	3 acres
do	2s. 6d. rent	from 1653	2 acres

Not in Survey

Glebe land

1759 Estate Map and Notes from Survey Book of c.1743

Tenants listed are for c.1724

A Map of the Manors of East Preston and Kingston near Arundel in the County of Sussex belonging to Jam' Colebrooke Esq. Taken from a survey of Messrs Smyth and Brown by Samuel Wilkinson AD 1759

[1724 tenants]		[1743 tenants]	
A Widow Hammond	Manor Hse	Thomas Lulham	21 years from 1742 at £98 pa
B Thomas May	Baytree Hse	Thomas May	21 years from 1742 at £98 pa
C James South	Forge Cottage	Ann South	copyhold at 22s. pa
D William Wolvin	Rosery	Charles Hill	lease at £12 pa
E Elizabeth Ingram	Wistaria	John Ingram	copyhold at 6s. pa

Freeholders paying quit rent

F Elizabeth Dean	Homestead	Richard Holmes	copyhold at 10s.
	Homestead	Richard Holmes	freeholds at 9s. 7d. rent
G William Richardson	Old Yews	William Richardson	freehold at 18d. pa
H John Baker	Baytree Cottage	John Baker	freehold at 16d. pa
I Thomas Greatwick Esq.	land	Thomas Gratwick Esq.	freehold at 20d. pa

Freeholders paying no quit rent

K Mr Robotham	Beehives	Oliver Penfold	21 year lease from 1742 at £48 pa
L Elizabeth Hettly	Corner House	John Mounshire	freehold no rent

MMr Green	House on Bend	John Barnet	freehold no rent
I Thomas Greatwick Esq.	land	William Gratwick	freehold no rent
N Widow Wintor	Winters	John Close	freehold no rent
O William Clare	Boxtree Cottage	James Baker	freehold no rent
P Church Land	Glebe	Church land	freehold no rent

The Tenants of the Manor of Kingston

| Q Thomas Oliver | Manor Hse | William Olliver | 21 years from 1742 at £222 |
| B Thomas May | … | Thomas May | included in Baytrees |

Copyholders

R William Oliver	[West Kingston]	William Olliver	copyhold at 39s. 4d.
S John Bennett	[house]	William Olliver	with manor farm
H John Baker	…	William Olliver	with manor farm
T Mr Elphick	…	Mrs Elphick	copyhold at [13s.]
V Richard Webb	[houses]	William Olliver	with manor farm

Freeholders paying quit rent

| R William Oliver | … | William Olliver | freeholds at 6s. 1d. rent |
| T Mr Elphick | [Moorings] | Thomas May | included in Baytrees |

Freehold no rent

| W Ferring Church Land | Glebe | church land | freehold no rent |

In East Preston the farms remained fairly intact through the two periods, but in Kingston considerable inclosure and exchanges took place.

Rentals Extract, James Colebrooke Jun. Esq. 1743-44

Thomas Lulham Tenant P Lease dated 16th August 1742 for 21 Years from Michaelmas following to East Preston Demeans And also a Marsh called Climping Corner in Court Wicke. The whole at £98 P Annum Note this Includes the Tiths of Corn of his own Farm the £8 being for the said Tiths, Tenant pays Land tax not exceeding 2s in the £ to do all repairs being allowed Rough Timber And to allow the Lord or Steward to keep Courts at the Mannor House, Not to plough Church Field, Middle Pasture Alias Barn Field, Nine Acres Alias House Field and Climping Corner.

William Oliver Tenant P Lease dated [blank] for 21 Years from Michaelmas 1742 at £222 P Annum to all Kingston Farm, As also part of the Land late Elphicks, The Land late Bakers, and Bennets, in Kingston, And also 4 marshes in Week, The whole except the Marshes is Tith free in which is also Included the Tith of his own Freehold, and Copyhold Land in Kingston.

The whole Colebrooke estate in Sussex, including East Preston, Kingston, Wick, Barpham, Ferring Grange and various farms, was worth almost £2000 gross rent, of which, East Preston and Kingston were over £490.

Land Tax 1780

East Preston

Only the owners and tenants are named, with a land valuation, in the original documents.

Owner	Tenant	Value	Farm
John Corney	Geo. Wyatt	£82	Manor House
John Corney	Rich Wyatt	£8	ditto
Thomas Banks	Wm. Olliver	£16	Corner House
William Gratwicke	Wm. Penfold	£12	Gratwicke lands
George Olliver	John Simmons	£50	Baytree House
Joseph Sanders	Edw. Langley	£23	House on Bend
John Slater jun.	John Slater	£8	Old Yews
John Baker	Edw. Langley	£5	Baytree Cottage
Widow Baker	herself	£2	ditto
William Henty	Richard Wyatt	£36	Beehives
William Henty	himself	£11	ditto
James Goble	Edw. Langley	£48	Homestead
Rev. Penfold	himself	£15	Glebe

This was a long-standing government tax, and the returns survive for 1780-1832 because they were used to show entitlement to vote in elections.

William Edwards Inventory

A true and perfect Inventory of all and Singular the Goods Chattells Debts and Creditts of William Edwards late of East Preston in the parrish of Ferring in the County of Sussex yeoman deceased taken and apprized by Richard Shotcher of Littlehampton in the said County yeom. and Thomas Polland of Littlehampton aforesaid husbandman the seventeenth day of December Ano Dni 1691

	£	s	d
Imprimis His weareing apparell and mony in purse	02	00	00
It in the Parlor Chamber, one feather bedd, with			
the bolster steddle and all things to itt belonging	04	10	00
It four chaires, one sideboard & little table	00	10	00
It in the Hall Chamber, one feather bedd, with the			
bolster and all things thereto belonging 01	05	00	
It three chestes and one box	00	05	00
It in the Kitchin Chamber three feather bedds			
six feather bolsters one pair of curtains			
and valence and other things to the said bedds belonging	06	00	00
It sixteen pair of sheets and one dozen of napkins			
six table cloaths six pillow coats and other			
small linnen	06	00	00
It three chests one box one joyn'd stool and chair	00	12	00
It in the Brewhouse Chamber one feather bedd			
one flockbedd two bolsters with the steddles and			
other things thereto belonging and one chest	01	11	00
It in the Parlor one table eight chaires & one glass cage	01	01	00
It in the Hall one table and forme one cupboard			
four chaires two andirons and one still	01	10	00
It in the Kitchin eighteen pewter dishes twelve pewter			
plates two candlestickes and two porringers	02	10	00
It two iron potts one jacke two spitts one pair of toug's			
two pair of potthookes two pair of gridirons one iron			
candlesticke and other small iron things	01	00	00
It one brass furnace three kettles and two skilletts	01	10	00
It in the Brewhouse one brewing fatt one tunn one			
keeler one churn four tubbs and three bucketts	01	16	00
It one brass frying pann and one warming pann	00	04	00
It in the Milkhouse butter and cheese	01	00	00
It nine milk truggs two powdering tubbs one kneading			
trough and one little table	01	02	00
It in the Buttery thirteen beer vessells and some bottles	01	07	00
Without Doores			
It twenty three acres an half of wheat on the ground	14	00	00
It barley and minglers in his barne att Rustington	05	00	00
It four pair of working oxen	32	00	00
It tenn cowes and one bull	27	00	00
It seven two yearling and three yearling beastes	12	05	00
It eight weanyers	06	00	00
It one pair of fatting oxen and the hay	15	00	00
It thirty ewes and teggs	07	10	00
It four fatting hoggs and nine leane hoggs	09	00	00
It nine shootes	02	05	00
It two mares and three coltes	15	00	00
It wheate in the barne	24	00	00
It barley in the barne	21	12	00
It oates and minglers	06	00	00
It one waggon and two dungcartes	08	10	00
It two plowes three harrows with ox yokes			
chaines and other husbandry tackle	02	00	00
It desperate debtes old lumber and things			
unseen and forgotten	02	00	00
Sum	244	15	00

Appendix 2

REMEMBERING THE FALLEN

Names on the First World War church triptych (the dates are incomplete)

Ormonde Bennett	13th Royal Sussex	1918
Samuel Birchfield	Hood Batt. RND	1918
Frederick Bone	7th Royal Sussex	1917
Alfred Boxall	46th Canadians	1917
Ernest B. Boxall	Life Guards	1917
Thomas C. Braiden	9th Royal Fusiliers	1917
Phillip S. Candy	HMS *Monmouth*	1914
Arthur Challen	8th Royal Sussex	1916
Arthur Charman	7th Royal Sussex	1916
Gordon W. Cheal	Machine-gun Corps	1916
William A. Crebbin	8th Batt. Rifle Brigade	1918
Charles Denyer	4th Royal Sussex	1917
George E. Glinster	11th Royal Sussex	1917
Archibald F. Hills	4th Royal Sussex	1918
Harry C. Lintott	5th London Regiment	1918
Percy C. Newman	2nd Royal Sussex	1915
Bertram B. C. Newman	4th Royal Sussex	1917
William M. Palmer	7th Royal Sussex	1916
Stanley C. Parsons	HMS *Hampshire*	1916
Alfred Pike	9th Royal Sussex	1916
James Roberts	11th Middlesex Regiment	1917
Frank Standing	Royal Engineers	1918

Pte Alfred Boxall

Pte Ernest Boxall

Names in the Second World War church memorial folder (no regiments or dates)

Anthony Stuart Antunovich	Thomas Norman Middleton
John Shaw Bayliss	William Pitts
Anthony Compton	Nancy Barbara Richardson
Michael John Rance de Courcy	George Richold
Peter Craig	Audrey Eileen Welsford Smithers
Latimer Hugh Denison	Roland Songhurst
Charles Greenough	Richard Carrington Way
Thomas Russell Kirkham	Patrick Trevor Williams
Peter Sydney Lush	Peter Trevor Williams
John Henry Marpole	Malcom Henry Cathcart Young

Pte Fred Bone

These portraits are taken from the magazine Scribble *published by William Hollis. The names of their regiments, as he gave them, was not the same as on the Memorial in all instances.*

Pte Gordon Cheal

L/Cpl G.E. Glinster

Sgt B. Newman

Cpl P. Newman

Pte Roberts

NOTES

Parish Boundaries

1 OS Maps show the boundaries including Parish Boundary Sketch Maps *c.*1876, when John Haines was the meresman for East Preston and Kingston.
2 RDC takes over rife for improvements 1938.
3 OS Boundary Sketch Maps – 'by LGB Order No. 7429 dated 20 December 1877 all that isolated and detached part of East Preston shall be … amalgamated with the parish of Angmering'.

Local History Sources and Notes

1 WSRO MP3178.
2 WSRO MP157.
3 PRO Tithe Files Preston and Kingston IR18 10385 and 10443: Maps IR35 156 and 215: Apportionments IR29.
4 WSRO Add Mss 46765.
5 WSRO Add Mss 35808.
6 SRO DD/AH 3/7.
7 WSRO CapI/38/1. Richard Williams was steward to the Dean and Chapter but also to William Palmer for his manors of East Preston, Kingston, Wick, Donnington and Hulsters.
8 WSRO East Preston MP 2491: Kingston MP 2492.
9 WSRO East Preston Par 152 and E 152: Kingston Par 114 – church rates and other items survive for part of the 19th century.
10 WSRO East Preston Union largely under WG2/ … and WG9/ … Add Mss 2754 and 6281-87.
11 All of these journals are now at WSRO or Worthing Reference Library.
12 In 1602 Kingston had both kinds of copyhold, but East Preston only copyholds for lives.
13 WSRO EpI/25/1 1635 glebe terriers for East Preston and Kingston extensively noted.
14 WSRO Par152/9/1 in 1860 great tithe owners repaired the chancel. In *c.*1840, when tithes nationally were made a monetary payment, the small tithe for Kingston was £18 6s., great tithe £92 14s.; East Preston small tithe £40 10s., great tithe £215 1s.
15 Ferring prebendaries from 1341 to 1869 listed in Nevre, J., *Fasti Ecc. Anglicanae*.

Chapter 1, Domesday and Before, pp.1-4

1 The Domesday translation used is from *Domesday Book: Sussex* by John Morris, Phillimore 1976. Background history on the creation of Sussex is from *The South Saxons* ed. Peter Brandon, Phillimore 1978. See also an *Historical Atlas of Sussex* by Leslie and Short, Phillimore 1999.

2 Fowler, J. ed., *High Stream of Arundel*, *c.*1636.
3 SAC 98. Eight cinerary urns were found in Vermont Drive in 1956, presumably indicating nearby Romano-British settlement.
4 SAC 86.
5 Morris, J., *Domesday Book: Sussex*, 1976.
6 WSRO MD306 Rustington East Court Survey 1568, 'There is also … one salte marshe lyenge betwene the stonebeache and the fyrme lande conteyning … 100 acres … '

Chapter 2, Lords of the Manor, pp.5-8

1 EPNS, held by Hunfridus de Milliers in Pipe Rolls.
2 SRS 7 fines No. 522 John Maunsel settled on Emma de Fleming in 1251: SRS 93 p. 44.
3 SRS 93; L.F. Salzman, *Tregoz. A history of the family* SRS 7 fines. 759 Emma and Henry de Legh to Henry Tregoz for 250 marks.
4 WSRO Add Mss 31337 conveyance 1526; SRS 19-20 Fines.
5 Pike, W.T., *Sussex in the Twentieth Century*, 1910: 'From Dugdale … we know that Roger de Montgomerie … gave a grant of the manors of Kyngestone … and Wyke … to his daughter Sibel on her marriage with Robert Fitz Hamon [who gave the] manors to the … Abbey of Tewkesbury in 1102.'
6 WSRO Add Mss 31331 conveyance 1540.
7 SRS 14 IPM.
8 SRS 3 and 33.
9 SRO DD/AH … Fairfield deeds and wills; Collinson, *History of Somerset*, 1791; Sales of Wards in Somerset 1603-41.
10 Huxford J.F., *Arms of Sussex Families*, Phillimore 1982; SRS 19-20 Fines.
11 SAC 71.
12 WSRO Add Mss 830 Marriage Settlement.
13 WSRO Add Mss 52005 Elizabeth Shelley to William and George Olliver 10 February 1786, the whole of Kingston and several quit rents for freeholds in East Preston.
14 WSRO HC785 conveyance 24 November 1773 for £5,710.
15 1743 Colebrooke manors survey, Anon.

Chapter 3, Coastal Erosion and Population, pp. 9-12

1 Rudling D. ed., *The Archaeology of Sussex to A.D.2000*, 2003.
2 Brandon, *The South Saxons*, Phillimore 1978, p.9.
3 Rudling, p.13: WSRO MD306.
4 WSRO Add Mss 46862 Map of West Ferring 1621. In the

1490s Tewkesbury reported pasture and fields lost to the sea at Kingston, *VCH Glos*. 2.

5 The coastline in 1671 estimated from common field strips subsequently lost.

6 *Scribble*, February 1918, 'another acre of land has been lost making about four since we first remember it'.

7 SRS 10, the subsidy or tax rolls from 1296 to 1332, may be used to estimate population, but very approximately for small villages.

8 WSRO EpI/49/34.

9 SRS 5, Protestation Returns, 23 men over eighteen years signing the oath.

10 WSRO MP 3178: Par152/1/5/1.

11 EpI/26/4.

Chapter 4, Medieval Farms, pp. 13-18

1 SRS 93 Salzman, L.F., *Tregoz*, 'a beautifully written little volume' now in the BL.

2 SRS 2 fines.

3 WSRO EpI/25/1 glebe terrier.

4 WSRO EpI/55/46 Vice Admiralty papers, several Kingston and East Preston men presented for taking flotsam and even a shallop or boat, belonging to the Earl of Arundel as lord in chief.

5 WSRO CapI/38/1 in 1618 a 12d. fine was imposed for pasturing cattle on the commons in the summer.

Chapter 5, Manors and Rents, pp.19-22

1 SRO DD/AH 3/7 Rental for 1607.

2 WSRO EpI/49/34.

3 WSRO Add Mss 31326.

4 Deduced from notes of individual strips being exchanged in the 1671 survey.

5 WSRO Add Mss 53724.

6 WSRO Add Mss 26558-876.

Chapter 6, Priests, their Houses and Farms, pp.23-6

1 SRS 46.

2 WSRO MP384 Goring and Ferring with Kingston – East Preston with Rustington in 1657.

3 SAC 5, Kingston chaplain named in 1380; SAC 61 Episcopal Returns 1563, Ferring a vicar and curates for both East Preston and Kingston.

4 SRS 36; SRS 14 Thomas Palmer seized of free chapels; EpI/23/5 in 1579 Sir Thomas Palmer patron of East Preston Patronage of Kingston included in 1540 manor sale to Palmer.

5 WSRO EpI23/5 churchwarden presentment 1579.

6 WSRO Par1/25/1 glebe terriers for East Preston and Kingston 1635, when Preston had a notional 13¾ acres, Kingston 2½ acres and another ½ acre in Wick.

7 Conveyance 6 June 1912 in Warren deed abstracts.

8 WG 12 April 1911; Parish Magazine 1912-13; temporalities from 1 October.

9 WSRO MP384.

10 WSRO Par 83/6/7.

11 Vicars of Ferring listed in WSRO MP 1094-9 from Bishop's Registers.

12 Calvary to his memory in churchyard dedicated 1936.

Chapter 7, Church and Churchyard, pp.27-31

1 WSRO EpI/23/4.

2 WSRO EpI/26/1.

3 SRS 49.

4 WSRO EpI/22/1 1641 Easter Bill.

5 WSRO Par 152/7/7 and Par 83/7/2 November 1912, Johnston P. FRIBA, architectural survey of church dated 1912 is largely trustworthy, although some windows in the nave are 19th-century copies of the 15th-century windows.

6 Parish Leaflets 1951, Par152/4/17.

7 SAC 57 and 62 describe the East Preston bell. George P. Elphick inf. 1985 re size of bell and weight from inspection of 1936: rehung 1956 as noted in church leaflets.

8 WSRO Par 152/24/2 sale approved for £200.

9 WSRO EpI/26/1; 26/2 is another report of 1636.

10 WSRO EpI/11/16.

11 WSRO EpI/26/4 and SRS 78.

12 WSRO EpI/40/27.

13 WSRO EpI/17/43.

14 WSRO Par 152/1/1/2 In the year ... 1792 the Roof of Preston Church was taken off and repaired ...

15 WSRO Par 152/9/1 notes stone for porch.

16 WSRO Par 152/9/1 south aisle added; Par 152/4/1 faculty; Par 152/1/3/1 register note.

17 WSRO EpI/22/A1 ministers article 1893.

18 WSRO Par 152/4/17 faculty.

19 WSRO Parish Leaflets 1962; Par 152/4/23 faculty; 152/4/11.

20 WSRO Par 152/4/12 land registry.

21 WSRO EpI/23/5.

22 William Walls bur. 1728: 94 old churchyard memorials recorded 1991.

Chapter 8, The Parish Government, pp.35-40

1 SRS 43.

2 SRS 5, I do ... vow and protest to maintain ... the true ... Protestant Religion ... against all Popery ...

3 WSRO QCR/2/3/W5.

4 Thomas Martin will 1613; SAC 16; Par 152/2/3 register transcript with 1676 note; SRS 78 church inspection 1724.

5 Report of Commissioners ... Charities 1819-1837.

6 WSRO Add Mss 31570 Corney Charity Scheme 18 August 1911.

7 WSRO RD/EP 24/2 pensions.

8 A substantial number of churchwardens from 1575 are named in church registers and in presentments EpI/22/1.

9 WSRO EpI/22/1 presentments for 1662 and 1673.

10 The compulsory church rate ceased in 1868.

11 SRS 49.

12 SRS 49.

13 WSRO EpI/11/3 small tithe dispute at Kingston 1576; Annales Monastici V, the vicar had £5 from Kingston manor house farm in lieu of small tithes.

14 WSRO EpI/24/92 Bishops Transcripts 1678.

15 WSRO EpI/11/21.

16 In 1982 the chancel again became less decorated, and the altar was made central in the chancel but not referred to as a communion table.

17 WSRO EpI/22/A2.

18 *Scribble*, 1917-19; WG 14 April 1914; Par 83/7/2 September 1913 onwards; Par 152/14/1, 2 rood in 1927; Church leaflets 1970, retirement of the Rev. Fincham, the Bishop defends ritual.

19 WSRO Par 152/14/1, 2 PCC Minutes.

Chapter 9, Farmhouses and Farming Life, pp.41-66

1 WSRO E179/191/410 part 2 Hearth Tax 1670; EpI/26/4

church inspection 1724.

2 SRS 56 Subsidy Roll for 1524.

3 WSRO EpI/11/16.

4 WSRO RD/EP 18/1A plans 369.

5 WSRO 1840 tithe maps and apportionments.

6 WSRO HC785 abstract conveyance John Bagnall to John Corney 24 November 1773; Add Mss 15985 and 52002 Corney deeds for release of interest in East Preston Farm.

7 WSRO Add Mss 52004 conveyance 23 November 1773; Add Mss 51999 conveyance 26 August 1802.

8 WSRO HC 1046 HC1113.

9 WSRO CCC 36 p.219.

10 WSRO conveyance 13 November 1865 in Add Mss 26573.

11 WSRO HC785.

12 WSRO Add Mss 6282.

13 WSRO Add Mss 31326.

14 WSRO Ep1/25/1 'John Lidford … his third hollybread lyeth on the south side of Stafford Wyses house … '

15 Boxtree deeds abstracts 1642-1926.

16 WSRO A. Dean 13.

17 WSRO Angmering deeds 1661 uncatalogued.

18 Deeds abstract 1869 reciting Richard Baker will.

19 WSRO CapI/38/1 round estimates for some Preston farm areas, perhaps deriving from old parts of a hide, in 1621: Thomas Green of Upmarden 80 acres, Edward Ride of Ewhurst 60 acres, Thomas Green 40 acres, John Rose 2 acres, Roger Gratwick 20 acres, and William Parker 8 acres.

20 WSRO Add Mss 830.

21 WSRO Add Mss 51998 conveyances 1797 to 1835.

22 WSRO A Dean 22.

23 WSRO Add Mss 51997, 52000, 52003, 52008, conveyances 1648 to 1812.

24 SRS 56.

25 SRS 19, 20 fines; PRO Prob 11/1509 G. Olliver will 1810.

26 WSRO CapI/38/1 In 1620 the steward reported, 'the sea hath devoured the way which the tenants had to the west feild' and a new footpath was agreed. In fact, a 19th-century path to East Preston had a bend in Kingston Street where it had probably been diverted north.

27 WSRO Add Mss 8755 Palmer to Lucas 1689.

28 WSRO HC 524.

29 WSRO Add Mss 52004 23 November 1773.

30 WSRO CapI/38/1.

Chapter 10, Olliver and Warren, pp.67-70

1 Smail, H., Courtlands, 1952.

2 WSRO Par 152/4/3 Warren faculty.

Chapter 11, Gilbert Union to RDC, pp.71-6

1 PRO C543 and C247 Parliamentary reports on the workhouse in 1843 and 1844 are quoted in this chapter, and general workhouse records.

2 WSG 21 May 1857.

3 WSRO Add Mss 2755 Order reconstituting Union 29 September 1869.

4 WSRO RD/EP 1/2 minutes; RD/EP 18/1A plans 183.

5 The carnival raised funds for the hospitals, and a fund for Littlehampton hospital was named after Miriam Gent of East Preston (Scribble, and plaque at hospital 1916).

6 Hutchinson, M., The Story of St Bridget's Cheshire Home,

1995, conveyance 21 November 1954, move to Rustington 26 March 1987.

7 WG 10 January 1895.

8 WSRO Par 152/40/1 surveyor.

9 WSRO RD/EP 18/1A the earliest by-law plans.

10 WSRO WG9/13/12.

Chapter 12, Coast Blockade to Coastguards, pp.77-80

1 Philp, R., The Coast Blockade, 1999; Webb, W., Coastguard, 1976.

2 WSRO Add Mss 52001.

3 PRO Adm 175/5-6.

4 Harper, C., The Smugglers, 1923.

5 WSRO MP3178.

6 WSG 8 October 1863, four men drowned on boat trip – Kingston men launched their galley.

7 Parish Council began to permit Sunday bowls and cricket in 1940s.

8 Abstract of deeds 1937, relating back to George Olliver will 1861.

Chapter 13, The Labourers' Revolt and Bushby, pp.81-4

1 Standing, R.W., Reading Writing and Riot, 1998.

2 Hobsbawm, E.J., Captain Swing, 1969.

3 Brighton Herald 20 November 1830.

4 Sussex Advertiser November 1830.

5 PRO HO 52/10 295-6, 299-300.

6 WSRO QRW758.

7 PRO HO 52/10 299.

8 Brighton Herald, 25 December 1830.

9 Sussex County Magazine 1937.

10 Brighton Herald, 1 January 1831.

11 Brighton Herald, 8 January 1831.

12 WSRO HC 19.

13 Rustington WI book 1947, quoting Mrs Day.

Chapter 14, The Schools, pp.85-92

1 Standing, R.W., Reading Writing and Riot, 1998; E152/12/1-4 log books from 1874 in particular.

2 WSRO Par 152/6/5 donations 1822; in 1818 a small school was kept by a woman for 14 children, Select Committee on Education report.

3 WSRO Add Mss 31572 copy of Charity Commission draft deed.

4 WSRO EpI/22/A2.

5 WSRO E152/8/8, 9 accounts; Add Mss 31573-75 copy deeds from solicitors.

6 WSRO EpI/22/A2 Ministers Article 1850.

7 National Society letters November 1871.

8 WSRO Add Mss 31572-75 Copies of Trust Deeds of East Preston School from Fitzhugh Eggar & Port; Par 152/25/3; National Society letters 1898.

9 WSRO E 152/8/1 Inspectors reports on school 1874-1915.

10 WSRO school log book 12 July 1887.

11 WSRO Parish Council minutes 21 July 1925.

12 WSRO E152/8/1 report 1904.

13 National Society letters 1934-38.

14 Church Leaflets 1937; school log book 11 November 1939.

15 Goatcher, H., oral history.

16 Under the Rev. Williams many Saints Days were observed.

17 Morley, E., oral history 1989.
18 WSRO E152/19/9 opening of new school 12 December 1951; Official Opening proceedings WSCC Education Committee.
19 Stromwall, D.E., *West Preston Manor School*, nd.15 (Endnotes).

Chapter 15, A Victorian Village & its Houses, pp.93-112

1 WSRO QDP/W85 railway plan 1843.
2 WSRO RD/EP 1/2 minutes; Kellett, N.A., *The Tramways of Littlehampton and Worthing*, 1990; WSRO QDP/W220 tramway plan 1903; Turnpike road plan 1825, 1828 and 1834 WSRO QDP/W54, 60, 67.
3 Pike, W.T., *Sussex in the 20th Century*, 1910, notes house as built 1838; WSRO Add Mss 26564 'and an old messuage … behind the same formerly stood … known as Corner House Farm … '.
4 WSRO SP349.
5 Manor House deeds conveyance 24 June 1876.
6 WSRO Add Mss 26573 abstract conveyance 29 September 1863; Altered tithe apportionment 1864.
7 WSRO RD/EP 1/1 minutes: Par 83/7/2 parish magazine February 1902.
8 Parish Council minutes. In 1997 the Council still owned 62 street lights.
9 Auction 2 December 1970 over 4 acres but the 1906 nurses house was demolished in 1973.
10 WSRO Add Mss 6284.
11 Angmering formed 8 March 1925 HF003, East Preston and Kingston 1 October 1938 HF037 Conveyance 22 November 1949. East Preston has dated its anniversary from 1937 when the breakaway was proposed.
12 WSRO Add Mss 19367 Inventory of stock taken.
13 WSRO Add Mss 35316 shop plans.
14 Inf. Mr Humphrey postmaster.
15 *Scribble*, October 1917; Add Mss 6281 7 August 1917.
16 WSRO Add Mss 11097 plan of home 1932.
17 WSRO Conveyance of 75 acres in Add Mss 26573 4 October 1893; Tithe amendment 1894; Beehive deeds conveyance to Peter Langmead 10 September 1945.
18 WSRO SP1127 sale of stock 24 November 1892.
19 Graperies Nurseries and cottages deeds 1893 abstract.
20 *Sussex Weekly Advertiser*, 7 January 1805.
21 Deeds 1806 to 1932.
22 EP/RD plans 18/1A 389; RD/EP 1/3 minutes.
23 East Kingston deeds.
24 Taylor, M., oral history 1976.
25 WSG 10 July 1873 names Lighthouse Cottage.
26 Goodwin, J., *Military Signals from the South Coast*, 2000, probably a hut and in operation from 1795 to 1815, manned by a naval lieutenant and mariners operating a signal mast.
27 WSRO EP/RD 18/1A plans 100 Froyle Cottages, Mr Sharp built Meadow House 1919.

Chapter 16, South Strand & Kingtson Gorse, pp.113-20

1 WSRO SP1258.
2 WSRO EP/RD 1/3 minutes, improvement; two houses owned by Miss Mills in rates.
3 WSRO EP/RD 18/1A plans 6 for Manor Road.
4 WSRO RD/EP 1/2 minutes, houses for Miss Buttery.
5 WSRO RD/EP 1/3 minutes, Bungalow.
6 WSRO RD/EP 18/1 16 clubhouse.
7 WSG 10 April 1913; WSRO RD/EP 18/1 78 estate plans

1919.
8 WSRO Add Mss 19370 building contract book; Angmering-on-Sea deeds:
9 WSRO RD/EP 1/4 minutes; *Scribble*, February 1917, December 1916. It was supposed to be easier for travellers and post to find, using the station and sorting office already there.
10 Smallpox hospital scheme discussed in 1914 when South Strand was already being built.
11 *Scribble*, August 1916.
12 WSRO RD/WO 14/1-2; RD/EP 1/4 minutes.
13 WSRO RD/EP 18/1 plans 195.
14 *Scribble*, August 1916.
15 Sales Particulars in private hands, 20 September 1932.
16 WSRO 152/6/10.
17 WSRO RD/EP 1/4 minutes.
18 WSRO RDC minutes 1936.

Chapter 17, The Estates, pp.121-6

1 Schofield, A.H., *The West Sussex Coast and Downs*, 1929; RD/EP 1/5 1926 Joint Planning Committee.
2 WSRO estate plans 1933 K8 amended from 1930.
3 WSRO Par 152/14/1, 2 notes purchase of part of this land in 1930 to be handed over to the Dean and Chapter as patrons; Par 152/6/13 sale in 1937.
4 Wilson, R., Temple Church Choir notes 2004; Lewer, D., *A Spiritual Song*, 1961.
5 WSRO EP/RD 18/1A plans 42.
6 WSRO Add Mss 21089-100 Frampton.
7 WSRO RD/EP 18/1 plan 173; RD/EP 1/5 minutes, *Willowhayne Hotel*.
8 WSRO Add Mss 26573 conveyance 2 September 1930.
9 WSRO Add Mss 26575, conveyance 8 June 1932.
10 WSRO RD/WO 1/2 minutes.

Chapter 18, Arts and Crafts, pp.127-8

1 WSRO MP3178.
2 Datestones in house and EP/RD 18/1A plans 244, 394; RD/EP 1/2 minutes.
3 Owen, M., *The Crazy Gang*, 1986.

Chapter 19, The Great War, pp.129-37

1 SNQ 5, a shipmaster may have lived there in 1332; VCH draft also quotes authority for a port.
2 Lower, *Survey of the Coast of Sussex in 1587*, by Sir Thomas Palmer and Walter Covert, 1870.
3 WSRO Add Mss 2736; SAC 89.
4 Anon, 1989 oral history.
5 WG 2 June 1915.
6 WSRO 2nd Battalion RS Diaries.
7 WSRO EP152/4/6 faculty 1919.
8 *Scribble*, March-July 1919; Par 152/9/1 expenditure on previous organ from *c*.1886; controversially worded triptych installed 1922 Par 152/14/1, 2; information from K.F. Day church organist 1985, the old organ possibly by Bevington who maintained it, and notes on new organ including lettters from Rev. Williams family who owned it before 1913.
9 *Scribble*, December 1917; Par 83/7/2 November 1914.
10 *Scribble*, December 1917.
11 *Scribble*, October 1916, 40 soldiers from Littlehampton Hospital entertained.
12 G.S. oral history.
13 *Scribble*, April 1918, December 1919.

14 WSRO WG9/2/1, WG9/1/21 entirely handed over to military on 1 October 1918.
15 *Scribble*, various dates.
16 *Scribble*, April 1918.
17 Anon, oral history.
18 WSRO E152/12/3 23 October 1917.
19 *Scribble*, July 1917.
20 *Scribble*, April 1917.
21 18 November 1918.
22 Programme leaflet for village Peace Day.

Chapter 20, The Second World War, pp.137-41

1 Church leaflet November 1938.
2 WSRO RD/WO 1/3, 1/4.
3 WSRO RD/WO 59/1 has details of civilian casualties in the war.
4 WSRO RD/WO 1/5 minutes, canteen.
5 Gander, L.M., *Long Road to Leros*, 1945. Gander was a *Daily Telegraph* correspondent.
6 Information from J. Hunt; the 6in guns were taken over by 147 Special Independent Battery 1943 to 1945, after the Canadians left; Reunion Souvenir 1946 programme and notes, Major Bruce Glen, officers and other ranks listed.
7 Kemsley, W., *The Scottish Lion on Patrol*, 1950.
8 British Red Cross, 1940 report, Sussex/77 registered 19 September 1939; also Sussex/216 given as Kingston 24 July 1939.
9 Parish Leaflets 1945.
10 8th Royal Sussex, in command of VP/52 a military supply base.
11 There are several buried at East Preston, including two killed at Ford on 18 August 1940.

Chapter 21, Social Life, pp.141-56

1 WSG 1 October 1874.
2 Gill, W.H., *Songs of the British Folk*, 1917. Gill lived at White House, Angmering, and collected local songs.

3 Cawte, E.C., unpublished Ms, 1975; R.J. Sharpe letters and Mss.
4 Anon, *History of the Cricket Club*, 1960.
5 WG 1896.
6 Blaauw Cup inscriptions noted 1984.
7 SRS 84.
8 WSRO RD/WO 1/3 minutes, King George Playing Field Fund 1937.
9 Deeds 7 December 1962 for £10,000 from Mr Langmead.
10 Langmead Recreation Ground deeds 16 February 1973 for £100.
11 WSRO RD/EP 18/1 plan 77.
12 The Guide Association information 1994; the Scout Association information 1993. Both groups were refounded at later dates.
13 First meeting in Guide Log Book 11 October 1922.
14 WSRO RD/EP 1/3 minutes, Admiral Warren Reading Room.
15 Opened by Ernest Raymond, novelist, 18 January 1962; 1984 memorial plaque in library.
16 W.G. smallholding applied for 1915.
17 Datestone October 1931; WSRO RD/EP 18/1 plan 85; Conveyance 7 November 1933.
18 Rifle Range conveyance 8 March 1951.
19 WSRO Add Mss 31571 29 August 1942 as per Vesting Assent 29 December 1943; Charity No 283037.
20 WSRO MP3178.
21 WSRO EP/RD 18/1 plans 104; Foundation stone 2 June 1928.
22 *Scribble*, August 1917.
23 Lismore datestone 9 March 1935.

Chapter 22, From Village to Millennium, pp.157-8

1 West Kingston Residents Association bought the pond and a large area of other land in 1994 as a nature reserve.
2 WSRO EP/RD 18/1A plans 24 and 25

Index

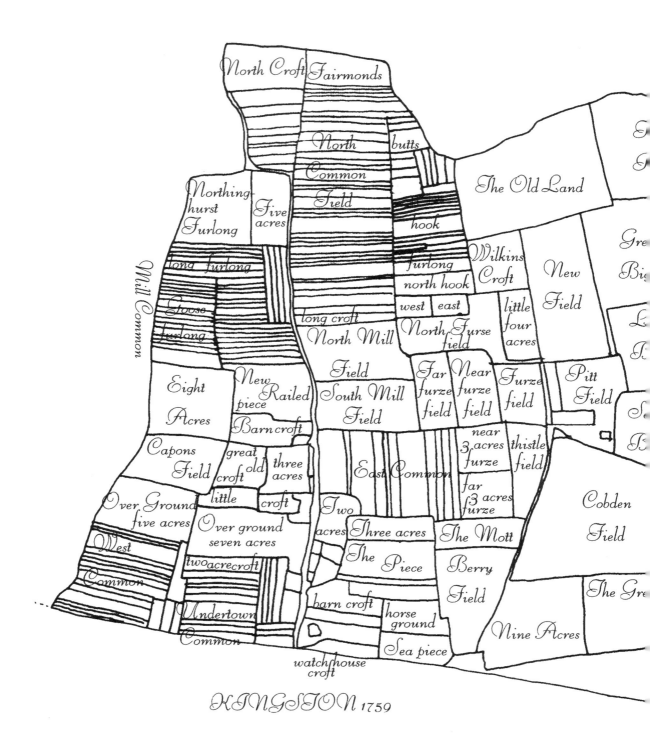

North Croft Fairmonds

North

Common

Field

butts

The Old Land

Northing
hurst
Furlong

Five
acres

Mill Common

long furlong

Goose

furlong

hook

Furlong

north hook

west east

Wilkins
Croft

little
four
acres

New
Field

Gre

Big

L

long croft

North Mill

Field

North Furze
field

Field

South Mill

Field

Far
furze
field

Near
furze
field

Furze
field

Pitt
Field

S

Eight

Acres

New
piece

Railed

Barn croft

Capons

Field

great
croft

old

three
acres

little
croft

East Common

near
3 acres
furze

far
3 acres
furze

thistle
field

Cobden

Field

Over Ground
five acres

Over ground
seven acres

Two

acres

Three acres

The Mott

The Gre

West

Common

two acre croft

Undertown

Common

barn croft

The Piece

horse
ground

Sea piece

Berry

Field

Nine Acres

watch house
croft

KINGSTON 1759